Charles Rennie Mackintosh

Charles Rennie Mackintosh

Anthony Jones

STUDIO EDITIONS
LONDON

Charles Rennie Mackintosh
First published 1990 by Studio Editions Ltd.
Princess House, 50 Eastcastle Street
London WIN 7AP, England.

Reprinted 1994

Copyright © Studio Editions Ltd., 1990

Designed by David Wire

ISBN 1 85170 412 4

Printed and bound in Singapore

ACKNOWLEDGEMENTS

On several occasions I had the opportunity to personally interview the late
Mary Newbery Sturrock, daughter of 'Fra' Newbery, Director of the
Glasgow School of Art in the 'Mackintosh Years'. She knew the
Mackintoshes throughout her life and vividly brought them and the period
to life for me. Isabel Stewart of New Jersey, USA, was also a valuable
source of witness to the world of the School of Art in the early years of the
century. My greatful thanks and memories. I sincerely appreciate the help
of Pamela Robertson, the Hunterian Art Gallery, University of Glasgow,
for her special insights into the life and art of Margaret Macdonald; Roger
Billcliffe, the Fine Arts Society, Glasgow, whose encyclopaedic knowledge
and scholarship concerning Mackintosh is without parallel; William
Buchanan, Director of Glasgow School of Art; Ian Monie, Librarian of the
School, and Peter Trowles, Mackintosh-Taffner Curator of the School's
Collection; Ralph Burnett, photographer, Glasgow. To those individuals and
institutions who loaned photographic material listed in the photography
credits, grateful thanks. John Wallace and Lizzy Bacon of Studio Editions,
and David Wire, the designer, I thank for their 'pluck, patience,
perseverance, and politeness under pressure'. My thanks also to Nancy
Crouch in Chicago. Last, but most, this is dedicated to my wife, Patty
Carroll and my son, Emrys

CONTENTS

The Mackintosh Style

GLASGOW 1900:
Charles Rennie Mackintosh and the pursuit of perfection

INTRODUCTION

"The whole modernist movement in European architecture looks to him as one of its chief originators."

Mackintosh's obituary in *The Times*, London, 1928.

The history of the arts of the twentieth century is littered with examples of individuals whose great works, renown and reputation have fallen into obscurity as fickle tastes and styles have passed them by, only to be rediscovered and reclaimed by delighted later generations. Such is the case of one of the most defiantly innovative, original and fervent creators, the Scottish architect–artist–designer, Charles Rennie Mackintosh. Touched both by moments of ecstatic brilliance and by the deepest gloom, his tragically unlucky life made him a star-crossed innovator whose work was appreciated by few in his native land, where he was reviled or ignored by most. His genius hopscotched over England to be recognized in middle Europe where, as the new century dawned, he was worshipped in Vienna for works that were icons, and ideas that were both prescriptions and prophesies.

Mackintosh was born in Glasgow, Scotland, in 1868 and died in relative obscurity in London in 1928. He was born in the middle of the decade, 1863–73, which spawned a band of architects and designers whose mature works constituted contrasting spans between the fading nineteenth and the dawning twentieth centuries. In that decade were born C.R. Ashbee (1863–1942), M.H. Baillie Scott (1865–1940), Talwin Morris (1865–1912), J.M. Olbrich (1867–1908), C.R.

Mackintosh (1868–1928), Frank Lloyd Wright (1869–1959), Edwin Lutyens (1869–1944), Henry van der Velde (1863–1957), Adolf Loos (1870–1933), Josef Hoffman (1870–1955) and Eliel Saarinen (1873–1950). During his lifetime, Mackintosh achieved regard, albeit briefly, as one of the most imaginative and idealistic young architects seeking to create a dynamic new architectural and design language for the coming twentieth century, and wresting that vocabulary from the cloying revival-ridden clutches of the Victorian–Edwardian continuum.

There was a new hope, symbolized by the arrival of the year 1900, and a burst of optimistic artistic energy, and as the twentieth century was born Mackintosh looked from that remarkable turning-point both to the real past and to the ideal future, fusing disparate threads to make a new whole: a deep respect for the architectural heritage of his own country; an understanding of the moral imperative in the writings of Ruskin and Morris; the ideas of progressive theorists (Voysey, Sedding, Lethaby), with whom he felt kinship; the discovery of Japanese architectural forms; and themes uniquely of his own imaginative invention.

In spite of the attention paid to his work both in Britain and in Continental Europe, almost all Mackintosh's buildings are limited geographically to the city of Glasgow and its immediate environs, and temporally to the prodigiously productive years 1896 to 1909. From 1909 to his death in 1928, most of his work can be considered only complementary and secondary to his principal architectural expression. Though possessed of an astonishing facility as a watercolourist and a furniture, interior and textile designer, his love of line, volume, mass and structure makes him first and last an architect, but one who sought in its varied expressions a holistic vision that would integrate and unify all the arts under the maternal cloak of architecture, "the mother of the arts", in the dynamic yet harmonic whole known in German as "gesamtkunstwerk" – "the total work of art".

In the closing years of the twentieth century the process of Mackintosh's "rediscovery" has involved a re-examination of his ideas and expressions that has been of particular interest to the "appropriators" in the Post-Modernist movement. As with many of the Early-Modern masters (Wright, Saarinen, Hoffmann etc.), the work of Mackintosh has been incorporated into the extended vocabulary of Modernism as turn-of-the-century design motifs have proved a rich inspirational seam for Post-Modernist miners. His furniture, silverware and textiles have all been the subjects of reproductions now widely available (though displaying considerable variations of fidelity to the originals, depending on the ability, loyalty or commercial attitude of the manufacturer). His writing desk of 1904, which in 1979 reached the world record auction price for a piece of twentieth-century furniture, has since been easily overtaken by works of considerably less quality. Ironically, for an architect/artist/designer whose inability to tinker with ideas and forms made him far from being a "mere stylist", it is the very stylishness and elegance of his time-validated designs that have made him so sought after.

Early life and education

"To understand both art and life one must go back to the source of all things, and that is to Nature."

Eliel Saarinen

". . . my pride is in . . . the architecture of our own country, just as much Scotch as we are ourselves."

Charles Rennie Mackintosh in his lecture "Scotch Baronial Architecture", Glasgow, 1893.

Mackintosh was one of eleven children. His father was a Superintendent in the Glasgow Police, of a Scottish Highlands family, and a keen amateur horticulturalist who instilled in young Charles the abiding and profound intimacy with nature that was to influence and provide inspiration throughout his mature life. Mackintosh was afflicted with a club foot, a drooping eyelid and a less than robust constitution. The traditional doctor's prescription for such frailty was physical exercise which, given the crowded domestic circumstances of a thirteen-person family, probably delighted Charles, who proceeded to wander the gentle rolling countryside surrounding the booming industrialization of Glasgow, the "Second City" of the British Empire. His instincts and love of nature, combined with an early-identified ability to draw, led to sketchbooks filled with studies not only of the flora and fauna but also of the buildings he encountered, which ranged from the simple expressions of vernacular architecture to medieval structures, castles and fortified baronial mansions. As he "thought aloud" on those pages, the logical amalgamation of nature with architecture placed him on a path he followed to the end of his days.

Notable in both the nature and the building studies is Mackintosh's confident mastery of line

1. Langside, 1895, *pencil drawing.*

2. Ascog, 1894, *pencil drawing.*

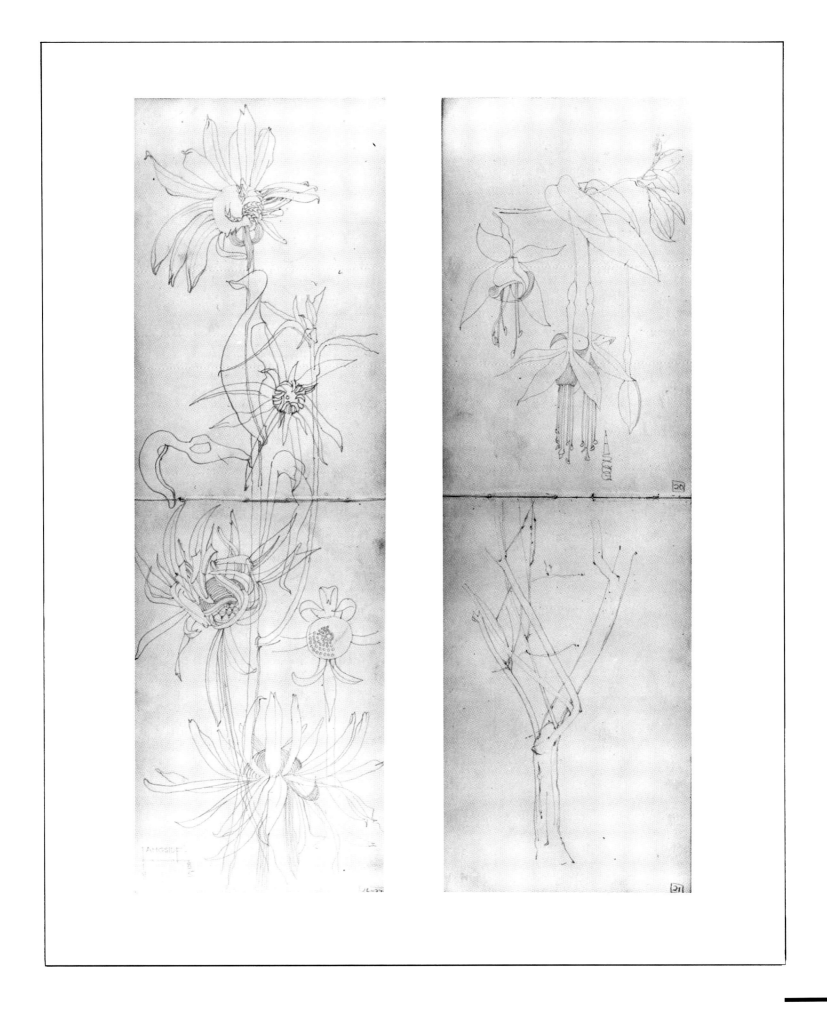

3. *Margaret Macdonald Mackintosh (1864–1933), seated in a chair of 1899 by Charles Rennie Mackintosh.*

and its application to analytical investigation. The flowers are scrutinized to reveal the structure that supports the forms, to create compendiums of abstracted designs that he would later employ in the very different context of designs for buildings, interiors, chairs, textiles and stencils. While initially his nature studies seem, like his drawings of vernacular architecture, to be about the creation of a catalogue of forms, the poetic and mystic power of the idea of nature as a powerful and

inspirational force for change gained strength in his work, especially as he became increasingly aware of the writing of Morris, Rosetti, Maeterlinck, Owen Jones and Christopher Dresser. The role of nature was of increasing significance in the creation of design. It was seen as an agent of inspiration, but Jones had cautioned against slavish imitation in *The Grammar of Ornament*: ". . . the more closely

4. *Charles Rennie Mackintosh (1868–1928) at 25.*

nature is copied, the farther we are removed from producing a work of art."

Charles's wanderings improved his stamina and his determination. He was considered a "lad o'pairts" (of great and various abilities), and he combined a pleasant personality with an iron will. We can only imagine the debate between father and son when Charles announced that he wished to become an architect, but his tenacity in adhering to his own beliefs prevailed, and in 1883, at the age of fifteen, he enrolled as a student at the Glasgow School of Art, a year later becoming "articled" (i.e. apprenticed) to the architectural practice of John Hutchison. Students at the School were expected "to give themselves body and soul to their work and submit to a rigid curriculum and course of study" that heavily stressed drawing and the study of the antique and historic sources, but which, as they advanced, allowed their personal interests to be expressed. Mackintosh attended the School as a part-time student for ten years, spending the early morning in class, the day at the Hutchinson offices, and the evenings back in the intimate atmosphere of the small School building. His work was commended for its "care and fidelity" and he was a prize-winning student throughout his years at the School.

The School's tradition of teaching was demanding and very direct: students had to prove that they had learned the skills they were being taught. Regardless of their eventual specialization, they were required to undertake a wide range of courses intended to stress their place in the continuum of the traditions of art and to hone their technical skills and demonstrate their mastery of techniques. The range of courses was wide, and Mackintosh's ability led to an expectation that he might be an artist rather than an architect, for he won prizes in diverse subjects: in 1885 a prize for Painting and Ornament in Monochrome, a scholarship which paid his tuition fees; two prizes from the Glasgow Institute in 1887; a bronze medal in a national competition in 1888 for his

"Design of a Mountain Chapel"; in 1889 six prizes at the School, others at the Glasgow Institute and a national competition prize for a Presbyterian church design. In 1891–92 a well-received design for "A Chapter House" (for the Soane Medallion Competition, in a Renaissance style) did not win him the prize, but when later submitted for a London competition won the National Gold Medal. His Gothic design for a Railway Terminus of 1892–93 was also well-considered, though the Soane Medallion remained elusive.

His specific academic architectural training did not begin until 1886, and thereafter the theory learned at the School was more effectively wedded to the professional reality of life in a practising architect's office. In 1889, at the age of twenty-four, he completed his servitude as Hutchison's apprentice and joined the newly formed architectural firm of Honeyman and Keppie, continuing as a student at the School of Art until 1894.

At Honeyman and Keppie, Mackintosh began in a quite junior position as a draftsman, though the exceptional quality of his drawing talent was early recognized by the firm. He was clearly an ambitious young man, self-confident, determined, rather opinionated, and loquacious. John Honeyman (1831–1914) was the senior partner, an architect with an established, solid reputation who was also known for experimentation and individuality. John Keppie (1862–1945) was very much the junior in the partnership. Only six years older than Mackintosh, he was less inspired, more pedantic, an efficient office administrator and competent architect. At first, Keppie and Mackintosh were firm friends. Mackintosh met Jessie Keppie, the sister of his employer, and it would appear that they became engaged: but Mackintosh seems to have eventually broken off this relationship in order to court and ultimately marry a remarkable young woman artist. Margaret Macdonald (1865–1933) was three years older than he, and of a rather higher social class, tall, red-haired and somewhat imperious. It is particularly unfortunate, given Mackintosh's later reputation of irascibility and lack of patience with his colleagues in the architectural profession, that in jilting Jessie his social and professional architectural career should commence on a sour note. Jessie Keppie never married and retained a devotion to Mackintosh throughout her life. According to Mary Newbery Sturrock, Mackintosh was "a debonair young man, tall, dark, and good-looking like a Highlander, with a fine moustache, and was photographed by Mr Annan wearing a tweedy oatmeal-coloured coat with a deep green Liberty of London silk floppy bow tie he liked to wear." Though in later years he was said to be taciturn and difficult, he inspired the enduring respect, affection and intense loyalty of those who knew him in these good years.

Flourishing Glasgow, the Empire's second city

"No more museum-inspired work! . . . instead designs by living men for living men . . . we must clothe modern ideas in modern dress, adorn our design with living fancy and rise to the height of our knowledge and capacity."

J.D. Sedding

"Great Glasgow, Dark Daughter of the North" was a large, smoky, heavily industrialized city, a major manufacturing and ship-building centre notorious for its Stygian gloom, pea-soup fogs, sulphurous atmosphere, and visible wealth contrasting with extreme poverty. Glasgow was not unlike other great cities in its desire to rebuild itself anew, using what its resident architects saw as both traditional and contemporary styles: Otto Wagner is identified in this context with Vienna, Antonio Gaudi with Barcelona, Louis Sullivan and

Frank Lloyd Wright with Chicago, Victor Horta with Brussels, Hector Guimard with Paris. The city that Mackintosh walked each day was, Phoenix-like, rising around the engulfed remains of its medieval and Georgian past to become a vital new Victorian and, later, Edwardian city: the recipient of a Beaux Art and Classicist training, he must have pondered on the erection of so much building in so many styles of architecture that had so little to do with the soil on which he walked.

In common with so many other cities of the late nineteenth century, Glasgow's architects practised as though under a spell, which, in a sense, they were. The enchantment was that of "history", the antique, and of stylistic revivalism that brought to Britain themes of architectural design that had no indigenous historical context or relevance to the country. The histories of "foreign" architecture were looted to provide new sources of inspiration for transplant architecture, and the century experienced endlessly diverting revivals of styles and themes from ancient Egypt, Greece and Rome, the Renaissance, Gothic, Medieval etc., with polemics and manifestoes attached (best exemplified by the salvoes from combatants in the "Battle of Styles", which set Classic against Gothic and which involved arguments about "seemliness" and "appropriateness" in architecture). Through personal observation and study, Mackintosh saw the vast majority of his contemporaries employing these architectural styles as being perfectly acceptable to Britain's compliant population, who devoured this feast of tastes apparently without demur.

His architectural training at the Glasgow School of Art and at Keppie's office provided Mackintosh with a core of theory and solid practical experience as he began to develop an architectural grammar that would be marked by his own uniqueness and individuality, in marked contrast to the stylistic conservatism that characterized the close-knit architectural profession in the city. While all the Revival styles abounded, there was a particularly strong penchant for the Greek Revival in Glasgow, its most forceful proponent being Alexander Thomson (1817–75) or "Greek" Thomson as he was known. His nickname was as ubiquitous as his works, most notably a series of widely published terraces and churches, all dramatic though slightly eccentric interpretations of his Athenian models. "Greek's" stature was immense, and, though they could never have met, and though Thomson's work and Classical exhortations would be set aside by Mackintosh, there is a connection between these two giants: Thomson had endowed the most coveted architecture award available to young Scots architects, the Alexander ("Greek") Thomson Travel Scholarship in the amount of sixty pounds, won by Mackintosh in 1890 for a pedestrian Early Classic Ionic-colonnaded "Public Hall" design. He used the scholarship for an extensive tour of Italy, via Paris, Brussels, Antwerp and London, in 1891.

Mackintosh's reading of the works of Ruskin and Pugin as part of his course at the School confirmed for him an inward desire to create a "new" language, one in which an essentially non-historical style stripped away the architectural associationism he was coming to despise and found "absurd". Pugin's comment that "architectural features are continually tacked on to buildings with which they have no connection, simply for the sake of what is termed 'Effect'" struck a responsive puritanical chord in young Mackintosh. A voracious reader, he devoured theory, example, polemic and poetry from a wide range of sources. He viewed with great respect the architects – in Scotland – James Sellars, James McLaren, and the towering figure of John James Burnet: and in England the work of the more radical practitioner–theorists like W.R. Lethaby, Norman Shaw and C.F.A. Voysey – "revolutionaries" seeking the symbolic touchstone of change for their idealized vision of architecture in the next millennium. While Mackintosh knew

and admired the work of Voysey, his feelings were not reciprocated: Voysey was known to dislike the practitioners of the Glasgow Style. For Mackintosh in Glasgow there came an increasing belief that, like Voysey's leadership of the English Free Style, he had to "eschew all imitation" of prevailing conventions, an emergent philosophy that was as current in Chicago as it was in Scotland. Frank Lloyd Wright, recalling that period when philosophical discussion and the mobility of ideas were meat and drink to the enquiring mind, observed: "Good William Morris and John Ruskin were much in evidence in intellectual circles in Chicago at the time . . . The Mackintoshes of Scotland . . . were genuine protestants, but then seen and heard only in Europe."

Mackintosh's Italian sketchbooks and diary chronicle the journey, the written commentary parallelling the drawings, for when he did not draw he wrote of his reactions and his feelings. The diary records the intensity of his emotional response to the Doge's Palace in Venice – "Such an interesting combination of objects, with regal scenery, transported me beyond myself – the custodian thought me distracted" – and his disappointment with the cathedral at Siena: "To begin with the whole front is a fraud as it gives no indication of the interior . . . the design is almost not there." The application of his belief in the logic of design, his study of the beliefs of Pugin, Morris and Lethaby in "ideas", "the real", "truth", "function" and, especially, Lethaby's dictum that "modern architecture, to be real, must not be a mere envelope without contents" took a firmer grip of his mind as he surveyed the historic models he had been taught about when he learned his trade.

For "Greek" Thomson and the Classical Revivalists, the architectural bible had been Stuart and Revett's publications on *The Antiquities of Athens*, but Mackintosh's interest lay far from that "old testament", in new "books of revelations", the five volumes of MacGibbon and Ross, *The Castellated and Domestic Architecture of Scotland*, published between 1887 and 1892, a comprehensive survey that confirmed his fascination with the vernacular expression and the architectural genetics of Scotland. Increasingly he came to believe that his countrymen had forgotten their own national architectural expression as they had come under the magic of Greece, Rome, Egypt, Holland, Spain, France, Germany – the styles of the south. Mackintosh looked south to England, and further south to those historic sources, before turning to look north, into his own country; and, in the company of the far-sighted few, he looked east for an historically unencumbered architecture, and found it in Japan.

Mackintosh, "The Four", Newbery, and the Glasgow School of Art

"It is a great matter for a man to find his own line, and keep to it. You get along further and faster on your own rail . . . and it is not the amount of genius or moral power expended, but concentrated, that makes what the world will call 'A Great Man'."

Janet Aitken in the Glasgow School of Art's *The Magazine*, 1893.

During his decade of studies at the Glasgow School of Art, Mackintosh formed a close and enduring friendship with Herbert MacNair (1868–1955), and they were both in the employ of the Honeyman and Keppie practice. Both had been identified as students of exceptional promise by the legendary young Headmaster (later Director) of the School, who had come to the post in 1889, Francis ("Fra") Newbery (1853–1946), a painter, educator and administrator of considerable ability. The School was in his direct stewardship, though under the ultimate control of the Government's

Department of Art, Science and Education in South Kensington, London, where the structure of the curriculum and required course of study were determined. Glasgow was considered to be a very high quality school, whose students' performance in various national competitions ranked it among the best in Britain, and in spite of the rote nature of much of the teaching methodology, it was nevertheless a fairly liberal environment that at least tolerated personal experimentation and individual development. Though on record as being "endlessly frustrated" by the curricular strictures legislated by London, "Fra" Newbery was a knowledgeable and more than sympathetic promoter of the newest trends in art, design, craft and architecture. Much of his understanding of these developments had been by direct observation in London before he came to Glasgow. He had the ability to find and encourage creative talent and originality and in Glasgow he found a wealth of home-grown Scottish skill which he nurtured and promoted. The School was quite small and located close to the heart of the city in not much more space than a large house. The staff were all recognized practising professionals who were expected to create and exhibit, and Newbery led by example. In contrast to the suffocating formality of much of late Victorian society, in the environment of a school of art there must have been some relaxation of such rigidity, but it still comes as a surprise to learn of the youthful Headmaster (he was only thirty-one years old) marrying one of the students, Jessie Rowat, who was later to become a notable practitioner and teacher in the revival of "art embroidery" in the "Glasgow Style".

Life in the School was lively and very active. Because the day and evening students saw little of each other, it was the ever-present Newbery who made a connection between the work and interests of two day students, Margaret and Frances Macdonald (Margaret Macdonald 1865–1933; Frances Macdonald 1873–1921) and the two evening students, Charles Rennie Mackintosh and Herbert MacNair, "Toshie" and "Bertie". The "laughing, comely girls" (Gleeson White in *The Studio*) had entered the School around 1891 when Margaret was twenty-six and Frances seventeen. An empathetic relationship, based on mutual interests in poetry, the Celtic World, symbolism, mysticism, and a shared idealism, developed into stronger bonds. MacNair married Frances Macdonald in 1899 and Charles married Margaret in 1900. These artistic and romantic unions gave Glasgow artists of remarkable verve and ability, known immortally as "The Four", creators of the core of "The Glasgow Style".

(The MacNairs remained in Glasgow until 1898, when they went south to Liverpool, where Herbert was appointed an instructor in Decorative Design at the School of Architecture and Applied Design, and where they remained until returning to Glasgow in 1906.)

While "The Four" were certainly a rather clannish quartet, it would be a mistake to believe that they developed work that was utterly contrary to or out of step with the work of their fellow students in the School, for their interests, if not their talents, were shared by others. There has been a mystique surrounding "The Four", hagiographers characterizing them as a sequestered enclave of modernist zealots, but in fact they were part of quite a substantial group of people (all associated in some way with the Glasgow School of Art) who were equally intrigued by new ideas and new expressions. Like "The Four", many read contemporary periodicals and books, saw exhibitions and heard visiting speakers – Walter Crane, Christopher Dresser and William Morris had all lectured in Glasgow. In 1890 a showing of works by the Arts and Crafts Society, brought from London to the Corporation Galleries, just a few feet from the School's studios, was "largely taken advantage of by the students". The Library at the School contained not only the predictable traditional volumes but also, probably due to Newbury's enthusiasms, more recent topical texts on art and design, including Owen Jones' *The Grammar of Ornament*, Dresser's *Japan: Its Architecture, Art and Art Manufacturers*, W.R. Lethaby's *Architecture, Mysticism and Myth*, Morse's *Japanese Homes and their Surroundings* (a copy of which Mackintosh may have owned) and Bing's *Artistic Japan*, together with the periodicals that revealed and debated the newest works and contested issues of the day. Jones and Dresser, and Patrick Geddes' magazine *The Evergreen*, were all concerned with the idea of art derived from organic forms and the Geddes publications with the inspiration of Celtic forms, "the melancholy power of nature", and suggested links between the Celtic traditions of Scotland's past and the present day.

The Glasgow Style

"In their own way, unmoved by ridicule or misconception, the Glasgow students have thought out a very fascinating scheme to puzzle, surprise and please."

Gleeson White, *The Studio*, 1896.

Although in the overall development of "The Glasgow Style" the indelible influence and greatest talent was that of Mackintosh himself, there were other innovators whose works contributed to the style. "The Glasgow Style", unquestionably led by "The Four", with Mackintosh's voice and vision the most persuasive, was a concoction of themes to which many were attracted. Though it was a loosely formed movement it was both identifiable and distinctive in its use of ubiquitous roses, themes of nature, literary references, mystic overtones and elongated figures by the artist–designers and craftworkers associated with the style. The works were in a wide variety of materials, ranging over textiles, embroidery,

stained and leaded glass, repoussé metalwork
in brass and copper, silversmithing, typography,
furniture, bookbinding, ceramics and illustration.
The movement was notable for its high number
of successful women practitioners and the School
of Art was so emancipated that it later appointed
one of these celebrated women as Director,
though her untimely death prevented Dorothy
Carleton Smyth (1880–1933) from taking up the
post. The youthful "Fra" Newbery promoted the
art–craft revival. A fascinating photograph shows
him in the painting studio of the old School with
a number of the talented artists, including both
Macdonald sisters (7). Chief among the Glasgow
stylists whose work received critical attention
between 1890 and 1920 were: Janet Aitken, Emily
Arthur, Muriel Boyd, Helen Paxton Brown, Ailsa
Craig, Peter Wylie Davidson, Margaret de
Courcey Lewthwaite Dewar, John Ednie, Annie
French, Margaret and Mary Gilmour, Alex David
Hislop, Jessie King, George Logan, Ann Macbeth,
Talwin Morris, Jessie Newbery, James Salmon,
Dorothy and Olive Carleton Smyth, E.A. Taylor,
George Walton, Marion Wilson, Jane Younger,
and a substantial number of others whose work
all contributed to the body of work that became
"The Style", and whose works met with
considerably more public acceptance than the
"extreme" expressions of Mackintosh.

Within the School of Art there appeared an
erratically produced periodical called *The
Magazine*, generally created by Lucy Raeburn,
"editress", which circulated among a coterie of
students of similar interests and persuasions, each
of whom contributed a page of prose, a drawing,
a watercolour or a poem before passing along the
volume to the next person to add his or her work
until it was completed and recirculated. *The
Magazine* was a snowball to which all "The Four"
contributed and, while much of the writing is
puerile and the artwork not much better, it gives

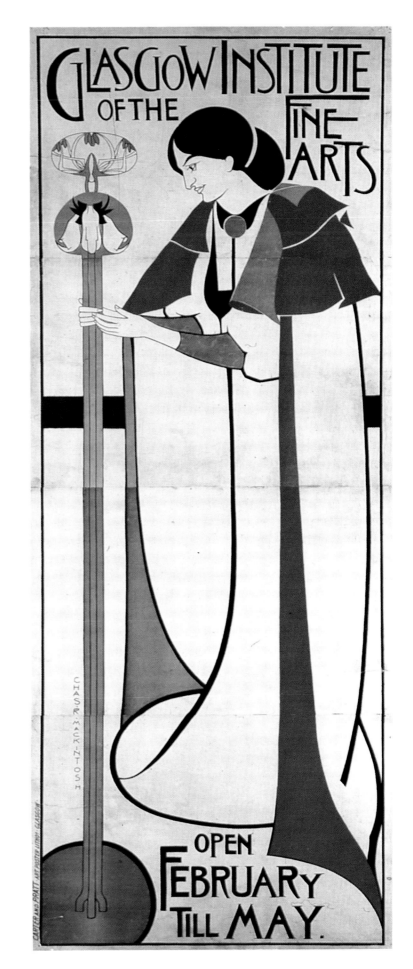

5. Poster for the Glasgow Institute of the Fine Arts, 1895.

an insight into the thoughts of the student–artists, reflecting their interest in romance, fantasy, literature and poetry, and revealing their determination to create a self-consciously "new" lyrical and ethereal style in respectful contrast to the painterly drama prevailing in Scottish painting of the era as represented by "The Glasgow Boys". The contributors' visual vocabulary concentrated on stylization of forms derived from organic motifs, and mixed attenuated skeletal human figures with leaves, flowers, butterflies, peacocks and roses. The first issue appeared in 1893 and *The Magazine* ran to eleven one-off issues over two years. "The Four" contributed a number of works, notably Mackintosh's *Cabbages in an Orchard* (7), the highly Symbolist *Tree of Influence* and *Tree of Personal Effort* (9), his drawings characterizing the seasons, and Frances' gloomy etiolated wraiths (28). *The Magazine* was a communication between acolytes, and its codes and references are now lost to us. It appeared privately in the School, in direct contrast to *the magazine*. The first edition of *The Studio* was

published in 1893, with national distribution from its London base. Its editor, Gleeson White, made *The Studio* not only a vehicle for unveiling the state of the arts to the British, but also a periodical that was quickly taken up as the most influential arts magazine of its day on the Continent and in America.

In Vienna, especially, it was of tremendous significance in the fevered debate over the arts, confirming, in the words of the architect Adolf Loos, that "The British are our Greeks: they are Nineteenth Century Man at his perfection." *The Studio* was required reading for ministers in the Austrian government and was to be the mechanism that created the beginnings of the Glasgow–Vienna design axis. In his important German-language interpretation of British domestic architectural design, *Das Englische Haus*, of 1904–1905 (in which he dedicates a whole chapter to the work of Mackintosh), Hermann Muthesius wrote of the immediate response to the Glasgow work which appeared in *The Studio*: " . . . the Scots received the highest recognition on the

6. Cabbages in an orchard, *1894, from "The Magazine", Glasgow School of Art, watercolour.*

7. 'Fra' Newbery (Francis Newbery, 1853–1946), Director of the Glasgow School of Art, in the painting studios of the School.

Continent from the moment they appeared . . . they had a seminal influence on the emerging new vocabulary of forms, especially and continuously in Vienna, where an unbreakable bond was forged between them and the leaders of the Vienna movement. England adopted a negative attitude to the new Scottish tectonic and decorative arts."

The Studio published the architecture of Voysey, the work of Walter Crane and Aubrey Beardsley – notably the "whiplash line" illustrations for Oscar Wilde's Salome – and the eerie drawings by the Javanese–Dutch artist Jan Toorop (1859–1928), whose The Three Brides (1893) chronicled an allegorical battle between Good and Evil, which contained emaciated and sinister female figures said to have been a significant influence on "The

Four", especially on the development of the work of Frances and Margaret. The elongation and fantastical anatomy of their figures and the ghostly colour washes they favoured inspired another group-descriptor among their critics: "The Spook School". A Glasgow newspaper had found their work so offensive that it implied that the police should be empowered to prevent such displays: it noted, "The ghoul-like designs of the Misses Macdonald were simply hideous, and the less said about them the better." These attenuated and "sleekit" figures were unquestionably a conscious stylization and not attributable to an inability to

8. The Tree of Influence, 1895, watercolour.

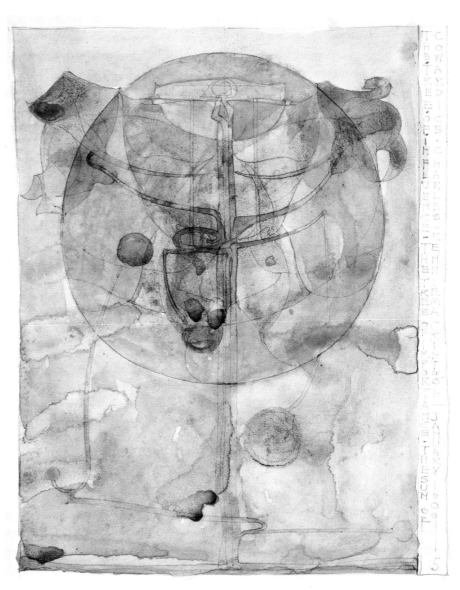

10. Autumn, 1894, watercolour, from
"The Magazine", Glasgow School of Art.

draw: Margaret, for example, had a First Class
Award in Anatomy Drawing. On this subject she
had told Gleeson White (*The Studio*, 1897):
"Certain conventional distortions, harpies,
mermaids, caryatids and the rest are accepted,
why should not a worker today make patterns
out of people . . . ?"

Nevertheless, the works remained a puzzle
with few clues: there was no "Rosetta Stone" to

9. **The Tree of Personal Effort**, 1895, watercolour.

translate and clarify the tangled meaning of their
designs. Their delicate mysticism, mannered grace
and sexual symbolism disturbed or repelled many
observers. Inevitably the maturing work of "The
Four" was seen as a Scottish reflection of Art
Nouveau and the "degenerate" Beardsley, but they
seem never to have associated themselves in any
way with that mannered expression (known in
Glasgow as "Squirm Style"). An independent
observer, Mary Newbery Sturrock, was to note:
"My father ["Fra" Newbery] . . . and Mackintosh
didn't like Art Nouveau. He fought against it with
straight lines, against these things . . . that are like
melted margarine." They certainly knew of
Nouveau, but they should not be too closely
identified with that movement: if they had an

11. Winter, 1895, watercolour, from "The Magazine".

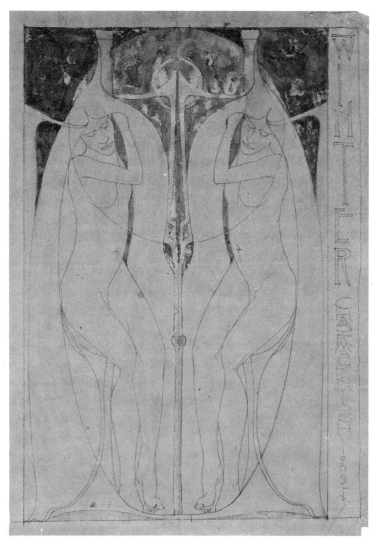

12. **The Harvest Moon,** *1892, watercolour, a gift to John Keppie, inscription dated October 1894.*

in 1900 wrote *The New Mission of Art: A Study of Idealism in Art*, was clearly in a good position to interpret Symbolism to his charges, to encourage and chronicle that new mission and to observe the radiant idealism of its young crusaders in his own School. In spite of their familiarity with European and English work, "The Four" followed their own lights and felt themselves untouched by influences. Late in his life Bertie MacNair said, "The work of our little group was certainly not in the very least inspired by any Continental movements . . . we knew little about these until we were well away on our own endeavours."

The lectures

*"There is Hope in Honest Error,
None in the Icy Perfection of the Mere Stylist."*

J.D. Sedding: the quotation became Mackintosh's motto.

"To be original means to go back to origins."

Antonio Gaudi

abiding interest in any European style it was in Symbolism, in both the visual arts and literature. The School itself was a fairly cosmopolitan place where, it was said, "there were always 'Continentals' around", and in 1901 the School even invited Jean Delville, a Belgian, to become Head of Painting. The Belgian Art Nouveau architect–designers Victor Horta and Henry van der Velde, and Guimard in Paris, were the most active proponents of the Nouveau style, but it was never to take firm root in Britain. Delville, who knew the Symbolists of the Continent, and who

On his return from the Continent, Mackintosh gave a lecture on his excursions, perhaps singing for the supper he had had by way of the "Greek" Thomson prize. Some of his drawings had already been exhibited to acclaim: the Chairman of the School's Board, Sir James Guthrie, said to the Director, "Hang it, Newbery, this chap should be an artist!" (rather than an architect).

While older source material was a powerful influence, Mackintosh was also aware of the work of contemporary artists and architects, but in his revealing lectures in Glasgow in 1891, 1893 and 1895, he drew together the threads of his own ideas. In his first lecture, which concentrated on "Scotch Baronial Architecture", he reminded the audience (either the Glasgow School of Art or the Glasgow Architectural Association) of the

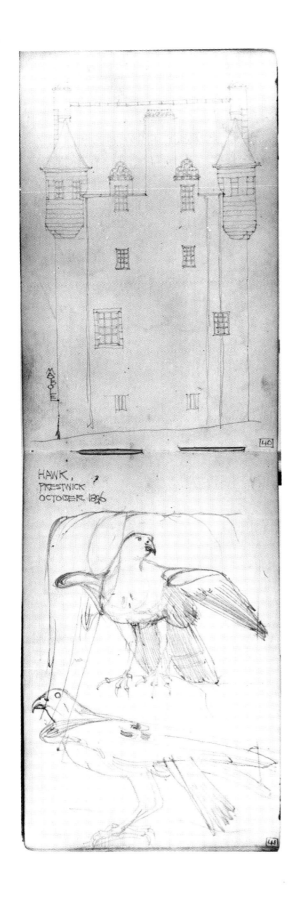

importance of their roots, and applauded with enthusiasm the interest then being taken by other architects in Scotland in the Baronial Style (Dunn, Watson, and MacLaren), whose works were a springboard for his own leap forward. He scolded his listeners for having neglected their heritage: the very subject, he said, was one "which has never as far as I can remember been more than incidentally touched upon within these walls"; he revealingly describes it as "indeed dear to my heart and entwined among my inmost thoughts and affections", and expresses his belief in "the architecture of our own country, just as much Scotch as we are ourselves – as indigenous to our country as are our wild flowers, our family names, our customs . . . " History, architecture, nature and nationalism, all in one.

Yet these instructive phrases, declaring as they do his concept of an adapted yet contemporarily appropriate architecture for Scotland, come from a young man whose own architectural work to that date was almost non-existent, and that which he had undertaken was all in drawings following the prevailing conventions of Classicism. In spite of the inherent Classically-inspired nature of his academic and professional training, and his Scholarship visit to Italy (which he began a month after delivering the lecture) to see the great examples, his love for the architectural expression of his own heritage was a lifelong affair and his Roman holiday failed to woo him from it.

Travel became important to Mackintosh as a source of seeing, remembering and drawing. The Italian sketchbooks were filled with observations and details that Mackintosh would use in transmuted forms in his later work, but they seem secondary to the influence of the journeys he undertook between 1893 and 1898 in Scotland and England, during which he filled his drawing books with subjects less grand than those of his Italian studies: close observation of more modest

13. Maybole Castle and Hawk, Prestwick, 1896, pencil drawing.

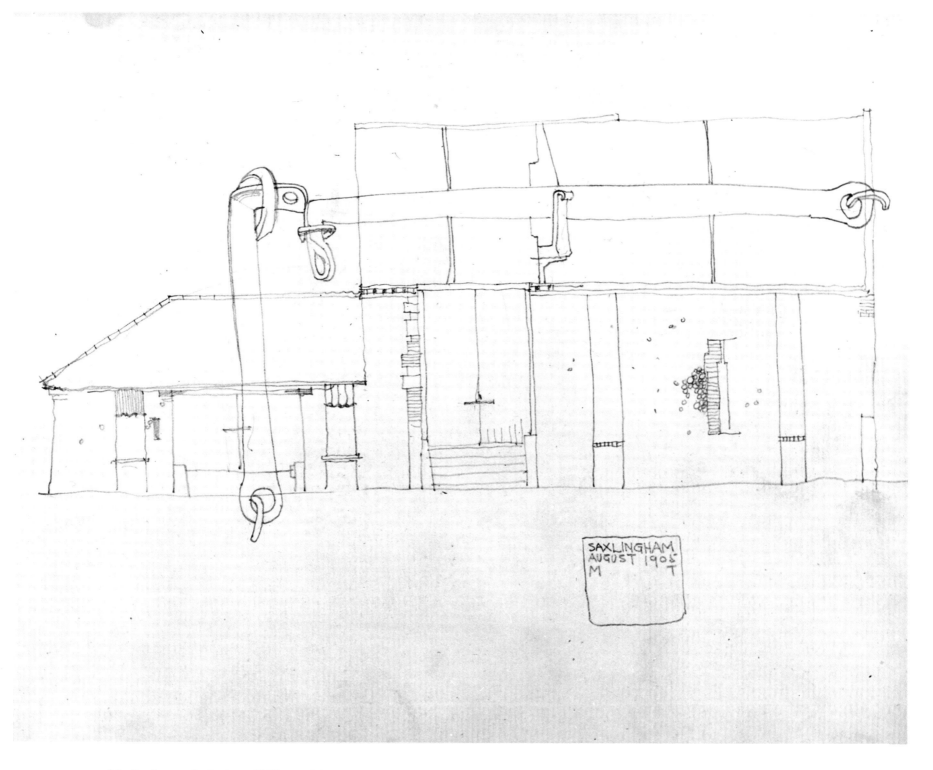

SAXLINGHAM
AUGUST 1905
M   T

14. *Oasthouses, Saxlingham, 1905, pencil drawing.*

structures, small churches, taverns, picturesque shops, manor houses and barns; and many, many details of doors, stonework, arches, windows, locks, hinges etc., often on the same page in an almost unreadable jumble as he drew plans, elevations, through-sections and details alongside or over one another. He concentrated on aspects of the vernacular architectural expression that was the traditional work of skilled builders, not famous architects, natural craftsmen whose simple

15. *Barn Saxlingham, 1905, pencil drawing.*

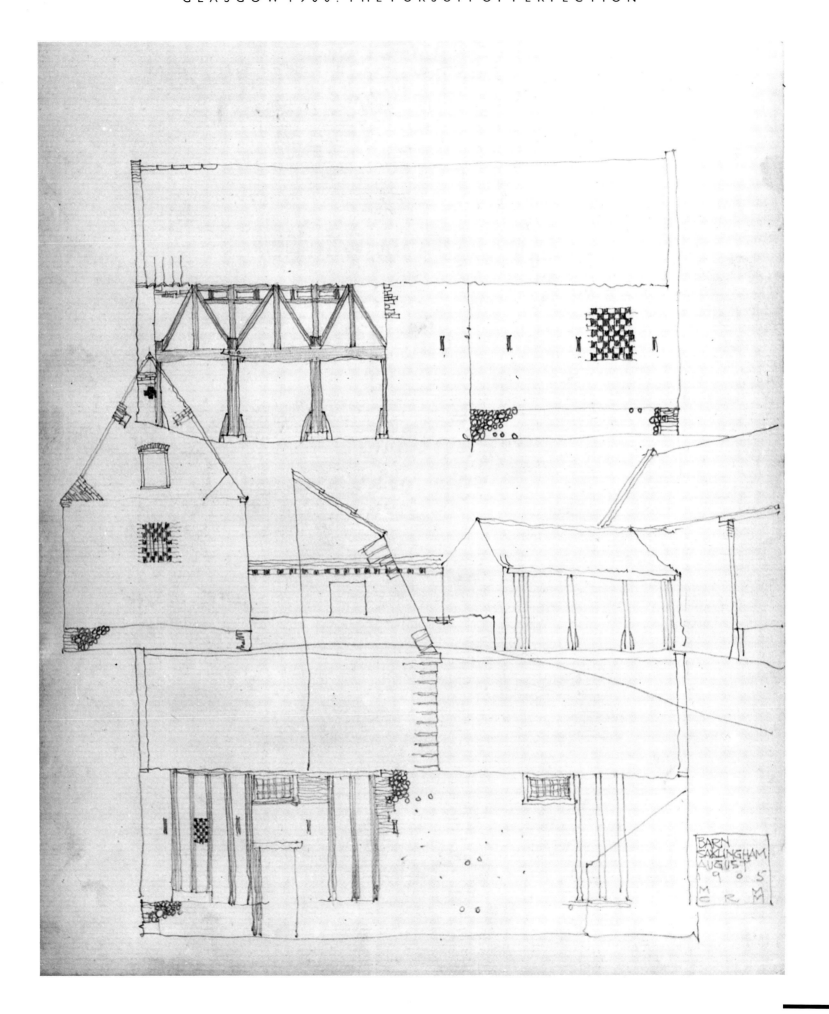

buildings rose eloquently from their unlettered hands. Close examination of the sketchbooks reveals the source of motifs and forms that are amalgamated into later works: the staircase towers at The Hill House (1904) and Scotland

Street School (1906) derive from his study of Falkland Palace; his small inn at Lennoxtown (1895) is a recollection of the Rising Sun Inn at Wareham; the windows of houses in Lyme Regis and Chipping Camden reappear in the central

16. *St. Cuthbert's Church, Holy Island, 1901, pencil drawing.*

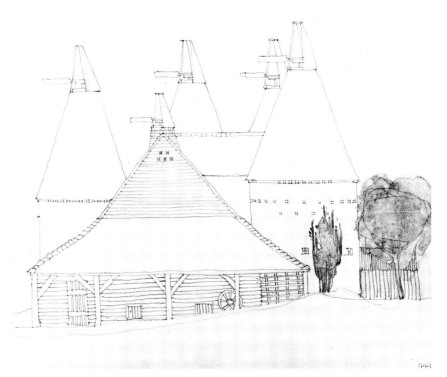

17. *Oasthouses, pencil.*

19. *A house, Groombridge, Sussex, 1909, pencil drawing.*

18. *The Dorset Arms, Withyham, Sussex, 1909, pencil drawing.*

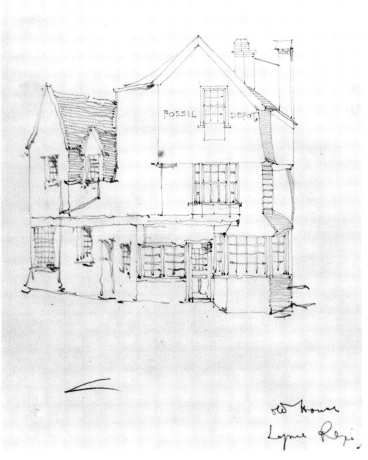

20. *The Fossil Depot, Lyme Regis, 1895, pencil drawing.*

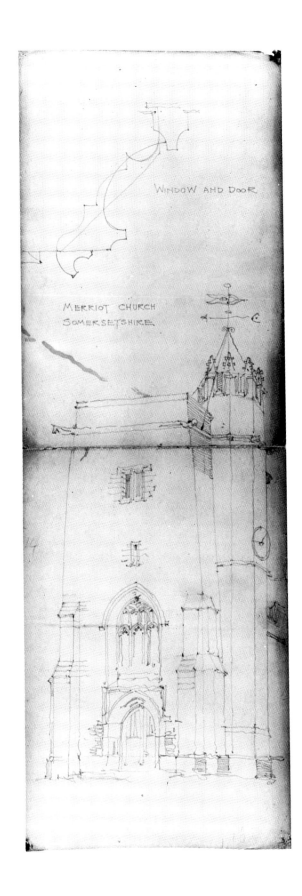

WINDOW AND DOOR

MERRIOT CHURCH SOMERSETSHIRE

entrance block of the Glasgow School of Art (1897); the tower of Merriott Church in Somerset translates into the tower of his Queen's Cross Church (1898); and the tower of the Glasgow Herald building (1894) derives from the Campanile of Palazzo del Rogione, Verona.

The 1893 lecture shamelessly plagiarized W.R. Lethaby's baffling and esoteric book *Architecture, Mysticism and Myth* (1892), but it again reveals Mackintosh's efforts not only to keep abreast of the latest ideas and expressions, but also to look beyond the endless trivial debates about parochial issues to the grander themes of philosophy, ideology and, most significantly, the symbolic aspects of architectural expression. Given the kind of painting and graphic work he and "The Four" were creating, it is understandable that Mackintosh saw Lethaby's plea for modernism as a clarion call to the possibility of uniting their two-dimensional symbolistic work with a three-dimensional expression: "Architecture is the world of art and as it is everything visible and invisible that makes the world, so it is the arts and crafts and industries that make architecture . . . architecture is the synthesis of the fine arts, the commune of all the crafts." The beliefs of Lethaby and Sedding must have been music to Mackintosh's ears: "We must clothe modern ideas with modern dress and adorn our designs with living fancy. We shall have designs by living men for living men . . . old architecture lived because it had a purpose: modern architecture, to be real, must not be a mere envelope without contents." Lethaby had written: "At the heart of ancient building there was wonder, magic and symbolism; the motive of our [buildings] must be human service, intelligible structure and verifiable science." Unlike Mackintosh, Lethaby seemed unable to carry out his own instructions: he founded and was appointed Principal of the Central School of Art, London, in 1896, and stopped practising as an

21. Merriot Church, Somerset, 1895, pencil drawing.

22. *Glasgow Herald building, 1894, perspective elevation, pen and ink.*

there are men such as Norman Shaw, John Bentley, John Belcher, Mr Bodley, Leonard Stokes, and the late J.D. Sedding – names most of you will never have heard before, but for all that quite as great if not greater artists than the best living painters, men who more and more are freeing themselves from correct antiquarian detail and who go straight to Nature."

These revealing extracts point to Mackintosh's familiarity (albeit second-hand, by way of the pages of the contemporary periodicals) with architects in the south and their beliefs in the creation of a new vocabulary progressing from, but not overwhelmed by, historical forms, and he joined their ideas with the deep undercurrent of Scottishness in his own thinking. He saw Revivalism in Glasgow as "absurd" and drew an exotic analogy: "All the great and living architecture has been the direct expression of the needs and beliefs of Man at the time of its creation. How absurd it is to see modern churches, theatres, banks, all made in imitation of Greek temples. There are many such buildings in Glasgow but to me they are as cold and lifeless as the cheek of a dead Chinaman."

Early experiments

architect in 1904, writing that he "did not have the technical skills or even the heart to meet the challenges of the twentieth century". Mackintosh, on the other hand, sought those challenges and tried to reconcile the "motives" of Lethaby within his own architectural vocabulary. Neither did he subscribe to Lethaby's belief that there was "an impassable gulf between all ancient art and our own".

At the risk of sounding arrogant, Mackintosh chided his audience: "I am glad to think that now

Charles' father, William McIntosh (who retained this spelling of the clan name, though Charles changed his own spelling from M'Intosh to McIntosh to MackIntosh to Mackintosh during his life) moved the family several times during the years of Charles' apprenticeship at Hutchison and his work at Keppie's, ending up in 1896 at 27 Regent Park Square, where Charles commandeered the basement as his secluded living quarters and small studio where he created both graphics and metalwork. He tellingly demolished a newer fireplace surround to reveal the old cottage-style grate with its plain surround

23. *Mackintosh's bedroom-studio, c.1896,*
with the 'cats' frieze, photographer unknown.

so reminiscent of the "everyman" architecture that filled his thoughts, and covered the walls with a fawn coarse craftpaper upon which he stencilled a frieze. This interior survives only as a photograph (23) showing an early cabinet of his own design, simple and well-proportioned, yet sturdy – and how tantalizing to see the spines of the books and how frustrating not to be able to read the titles that had attracted his interest! Above, and running around the walls, is the wide frieze containing characteristic motifs in the form of a slender

wraith-like female figure whose long tresses sinuously undulate horizontally to right and left below the ceiling moulding, and stylized cats beneath large round suns/moons. Bertie MacNair, in his own room elsewhere in the city, had also installed a cabinet of his own design, and had created a frieze featuring mermaids, the clan crest and symbol of the MacNairs, while in his room Toshie stencilled cats, the crest of the Mackintosh clan. Although they never actually collaborated it is clear that both young men embarked on exploring similar themes and perhaps set themselves subjects. The well-developed stylization of the figures and animals, the sun/moon symbol of growth and change, the use of stencil technique, show in this interior an integration and sophistication that portends Mackintosh's mature work. (The frieze was repeated a little later in the nursery at Gladsmuir.)

Of interest are the works of art that Mackintosh had chosen for his walls: some are too murky to decipher, but there are certainly examples of the Pre-Raphaelites and, unquestionably, two large Japanese woodblock prints in pride of place above the fireplace, offering incontrovertible early evidence of his fascination with the Japanese idioms that were eventually to be absorbed into his work.

Considering his lowly position in Honeyman and Keppie and his relative lack of practical experience (he had joined the firm in 1889 and was still a part-time student at the School of Art, continuing to 1894), it comes as a surprise to find Mackintosh suddenly designing and building two semi-detached houses for his uncle, William Hamilton, in Springburn, Glasgow, in 1890. Orthodox and rather mundane, they are easily passed by, as their external character certainly does not reveal anything unusual, impressive or strikingly new. Only the plan, taking maximum advantage of a site with good views, gives an indication of Mackintosh's hand in letting all other considerations be determined by the "reality" of the layout of the interior spaces – the "front door" is not at the front, for example, but at the gable end. In spite of its unimpressive exterior and an interior more notable for Mackintosh's use of strong colour than for the application of his developing theories of architecture/arts integration (the fittings were apparently bought from the standard stock), the reality of the commission and its execution provided the untried Charles with solid physical and practical experience.

In addition to his basement studio at home,

Mackintosh rented a small studio in the city where he could work after office hours. His friend Bertie MacNair had left Honeyman and Keppie to go into private design practice for himself and had also acquired as had Margaret, a studio–workshop; and in 1896 Frances had rented a small studio. Mackintosh's furniture designs for Gladsmuir, the house of his friends, the Davidson family, were probably conceived here, but most were made by the Glasgow furniture company Guthrie and

24. 'Redclyffe' house, Springburn, Glasgow, 1890.

Wells, for whom Mackintosh also independently created designs. The furniture pieces of the period are robust and rather monumental masses, but they have a wealth of inventive detail derived from the natural and figural vocabulary paralleled in his graphic work, to which were added wide metal strap hinges recalling medieval and Arts and Crafts themes, stencilled patterns based on flowers and peacocks, repoussé metal panels in brass, copper or scribed lead, and leaded glass panels inserted into the furniture, while the grain of the woods (usually oak or cypress), not silenced under a paint

31

or small suites of furniture. He had not yet found a client who would allow him the opportunity to draw together the architecture, interiors, furniture and furnishings into a cohesive expression of integration, but this approach is very clearly anticipated in his unexecuted 1894–95 designs for "A Library in a Glasgow House".

In the years 1890–97, Mackintosh's principal

27. Detail from the organ in the Music Room, Cragie Hall, Glasgow, 1897 showing carved naturalistic birds in a stylized tree.

25. Designs for wall decoration and furniture for Walter Blackie's principal bedroom The Hill House, 1903. Watercolour and pencil.

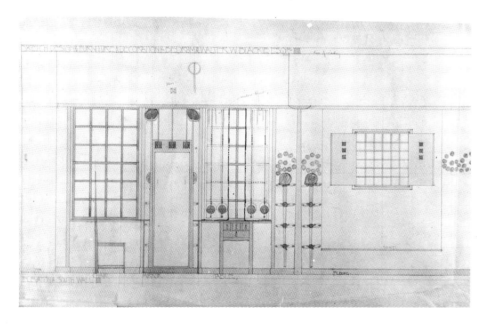

26. Designs for wall decoration and furniture for Walter Blackie's principal bedroom, The Hill House, south wall. Watercolour and pencil.

finish, speaks more naturally through stains and clear varnishes. All these works of about 1893–96 were, however, conceived as one-off single pieces

personal expression was in drawings, paintings, stencils, posters, furniture, graphics etc., which he created apart from the work he was assigned at the offices of Honeyman and Keppie. He was nevertheless able to bring some of those expressions to the work of the practice, and during the same period he worked with Keppie on the remodelling of the Glasgow Art Club (1892–93), alterations to the villa Craigie Hall (1893–94), the interiors of the Queen Margaret Medical College (1894–96) (78) and the new music room at Craigie Hall (1897), for which he created a spectacular organ case with elaborate stylized leaf and flower forms as wide strap hinges to the pair of doors, and a remarkable carving of a partly stylized tree with unambiguously literal carvings of birds nesting in it (27).

"The Four" in *The Studio*

Mackintosh completed his course of studies at the Glasgow School of Art in 1894, but throughout 1895 and 1896 "The Four" continued to be seen as a cohesive group. While still at the School they had, probably at Newbery's behest, shown their work together in a student exhibition, somewhat isolated and not mixed in with the rest of the students, in a declaration of identity that resulted in caustic ridicule from some and happy acclaim from others. Their work was included in a Glasgow School of Art exhibition at Liège, Belgium, in 1895, after which the Secretary of l'Oeuvre Artistique wrote to Newbery with an interesting compliment and observation: "Our schools of art are far, very far indeed, from being so advanced as yours and what has above all astonished us in your work is the great liberty left to pupils to follow their own individuality which is so different from . . . our schools . . . it is difficult for us to comprehend this freedom . . . that we admire so much." Newbery had evidently found ways to let the unique character of his students speak through the confining curriculum.

The sisters and Bertie MacNair had watercolours published in *The Yellow Book* in 1896 and in the same year (a year which can be considered the peak of "Glasgow Style" activity), due again to Newbery's connections, "The Four" made a very public entrance on the stage at the London Arts and Crafts Exhibition, where they exhibited beaten metalwork panels, posters, a large piece of furniture designed by Charles, watercolours and a silver clock-case. Their work was pounced upon by the critics and the public and subjected to a loud chorus of disapproval: it was identified, wrongly, with the Aesthetic movement and, worse, with the "unhealthy" influence of Beardsley, so they were seen to be offering an insult to both the ideals of Ruskin and Morris and to the dignity of nature.

The works were described as "the outcome of juvenile enthusiam . . . revels in absolute ugliness . . . a passion for originality at any price", and the derisive animosity that met "The Four" in the south effectively nipped in the bud the anticipation of the Glasgow contingent that a fruitful relationship could be created between sympathetic artists in the capital and innovators five hundred miles to the north. To this misinterpretation and misreading of the intentions of "The Four" there was, however, a remarkable exception: Gleeson White, the editor of *The Studio*.

This influential magazine's perceptive and inquisitive editor did not so readily scorn the apparently bizarre works at the London exhibition; instead he counselled considered judgment in a prophetic commentary: "Probably nothing in the [Arts and Crafts Exhibition] gallery has provoked more decided censure than these works, and that fact alone should cause a thoughtful observer of art to pause before he joins the opponents. If the said artists do not come very prominently forward as leaders of a school of design peculiarly their own we shall be much mistaken. The probability would seem to be that those who laugh at them today will be eager to eulogize them a few years hence." He was intrigued enough to go north to meet "The Four". It was to be a significant meeting, bringing together

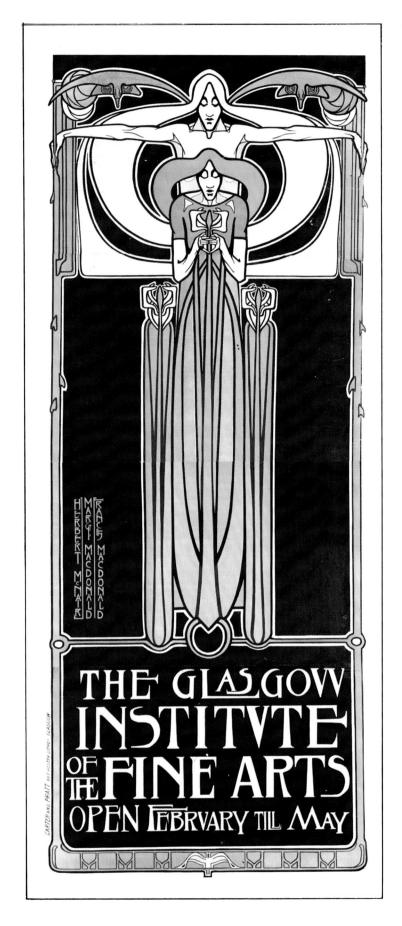

28. Poster for the *Glasgow Institute for the Fine Arts*, 1898, by Margaret and Francis Macdonald, with Herbert MacNair, lithographic print.

29. Poster for the *Scottish Musical Review*, 1896, lithographic print.

a quartet of inspired and radical talents with a man whose position and power could unveil and interpret their work with especial sympathy, which he promptly did. Just a year after the lambasting they had taken at the Arts and Crafts show the same unrepentant culprits were the subject of two major articles in the July and September 1897 issues of *The Studio*, which had the immediate and dramatic effect of thrusting them into a spotlight that was scrutinized as avidly on the Continent as it was in Britain. Thus, at last, the flowering of "The Four" in the relative remoteness of Glasgow was to be widely recognized as true innovation and the maturing embodiment of Mackintosh's "living fancy".

Glasgow, a "Tokyo" for tea rooms

"Now he who loves aesthetic cheer
And does not mind the damp
May come and read Rosetti here
By a Japanese-y lamp".

"The Ballad of Bedford Park", 1881.

"Miss Cranston has started large restaurants, all very elaborately simple on the new high art lines. The result is gorgeous! And a wee bit vulgar! It is all quite good and just a little outré . . . "

Sir Edwin Lutyens writing to his sister in 1897 after his visit to the Buchanan Street Tea Rooms by George Walton and Mackintosh.

In 1896, Mackintosh met the third of the quintet of important patrons whose support and friendship was to mean so much in his peaks-to-valleys life, and whose loyalty to him never wavered. He had already met two (though he did not yet know the roles they were to play in allowing him to realize his visions): "Fra" Newbury,

who was to commission Charles on behalf of its Governors to build the new Glasgow School of Art; and William Davidson, who commissioned the Windyhill house in 1901. Later, Walter Blackie commissioned The Hill House (1904); and W.S. Bassett-Lowke commissioned 78 Derngate in Northampton, England (1916).

Now, in 1896, came Miss Catherine (Kate) Cranston, a noted businesswoman whose faith that the Temperance Movement would rid the land of the social blight of "the demon drink" manifested itself in part by the founding of "art tea rooms" in her native city. "Glasgow is a veritable Tokyo for tea rooms" wrote the Glasgow wit Neil Munro, and Kate Cranston alone had several among the many in the city. What a happy coalition: the clever, determined and arts-conscious Miss Cranston; and the ambitious and innovative architect–designer, young Mr Mackintosh, both hoping to bring to their customers and clients the Japanese tea ceremony, Glasgow-style.

Miss Cranston's Argyle Street Tea Rooms had opened in 1892 and soon set a trend in the city,

30. Buchanan Street Tea Rooms, interiors, with George Walton, 1896.

room, to which she personally gave the closest supervision. Her new tea room expansion was planned for premises on Buchanan Street, and she had hired the architect–designer George Walton (1867–1933) to undertake the interior decor – Mackintosh's role was to be second fiddle to Walton. Mackintosh's principal contribution to the complex of rooms was a series of very large murals painted directly on to the walls, a frieze depicting pairs of side-facing female figures in long robes, interwoven with elaborate plant forms, tendrils, branches, leaves and shoots, interspersed with totemic stylized trees. The design derives from his watercolour *Part Seen, Imagined Part* of 1896. A halo-like sun surrounds each head, a recollection of the forces of mysterious nature seen in the earlier "cats" frieze, but these dramatic figures can also be directly linked to the poster designs and they have the same slightly strident effect of calling attention to themselves.

Continuing in his relationship with Kate Cranston and George Walton (before the latter moved to London to found an international architectural practice which, among other commissions, designed numerous shops and interiors for the Kodak Company), in 1897 Mackintosh took greater control of the design of the Argyle Street Tea Room. Here there was a clear division of work between Walton and Mackintosh: the former created the environmental screens and panels that delineated the areas, while Mackintosh designed most of the moveable furnishings. Among the furniture is a chair designed by Mackintosh that is one of the most unforgettably striking silhouettes in the history of design, a high-backed chair from the Luncheon Room (*33*), the exaggerated vertical stress and wide oval panel with cut-through stylized flying bird giving it a significant presence in the room, whether occupied or not. When seated in these chairs at a table in the busy restaurant one felt that they created a light, open screen around the table, to make a room within a room.

31. *Buchanan Street Tea Rooms showing wall frieze adaptation of 'Part Seen, Imagined Part'.*

though no one equalled her establishment, which featured excellent food and service, chess and domino tables, a smoking lounge and billiards

The importance of these experiments should not be underestimated. Even though Mackintosh did not have total control of the project the exercise was thorough enough to provide a

32. Part Seen, Imagined Part, 1896, watercolour study.

33. Chair for The Argyle Tea Rooms, 1897, height 137 cm., oak.

testing-ground for ideas he would bring to a fruitful and richly satisfying state in the Ingram Street Tea Room in 1900, and his legendary The Willow Tea Rooms of 1903. Already in Glasgow the names of Miss Cranston and Charles Rennie Mackintosh were synonymous, he the creator, she the provider, and the phrase "quite Kate-Cranstonish" became common in the city to describe anything new, elegant, refined, artistic and beautiful.

The influence of Japan

"Japanese art was the hobby of those in Glasgow . . . among the artists, as well as the dilettanti who could not afford Whistlers . . . "

Neil Munro, Glasgow, 1910.

The impact and understanding of the arts of Japan was vital to the development of Mackintosh's work. While he certainly looked inward to his own country as a source of inspiration, he undoubtedly loked to one other source and was subtly but deeply affected by the "alien" civilization of Japan. He was not alone in this, for the influence of the Japanese arts in Britain and especially in Glasgow is well documented. While Voysey, Beardsley, Whistler and the Arts and Crafts associates had all responded to the stimulus of Japan, in Glasgow there were a number of opportunities for the young and maturing Mackintosh and his friends to have had first-hand contact with Japanese culture in various exhibitions of 1878, 1882, 1889 and 1893. A knowledge of wood block prints was especially notable: and the painter E.A. Walton had even dressed as Hokusai to attend the Arts Club Ball in 1889. Glasgow-born Christopher Dresser lectured in the city on the arts of the Orient and had visited Japan in 1879 – his son Louis married a Japanese citizen and became a naturalized Japanese. The Library of the School,

the City Libraries and the Art Gallery and Museum all had books and objects for study; there was a Japanese pavilion at the 1901 International Exhibition; and two warships commissioned by the Japanese Imperial Navy, the *Chiyoda* and the *Sazanami*, were built in Glasgow yards in 1890 and 1898. Interest in Japan was so great that it impelled the painters George Henry and E.A. Hornel to spend almost a year there (1893–94), and on their return they lectured and exhibited to inquisitive audiences to rave reviews. Among many other articles on oriental arts *The Studio* published in 1897 was one on *ikebana* (flower arrangement), especially appealing to the Mackintoshes, and the legacy of this appears in the fantastic brambly twig compositions that feature in many of the photographs of their domestic interiors.

A substantial number of Japanese travelled to and from Glasgow; whether Mackintosh sought them out we may never know, but what is certain is that it was not in Mackintosh's character to rely on a superficial imitation of anything. Instead, he looked for and understood the symbolic and spiritual meaning in the arts of Japan, and in them found a new, historically unencumbered source on which to draw for inspiration, though not for imitation. While many examples abound in his work, note an early watercolour (*32*) showing a standing female figure among stylized flowers, the whole effect very Japanese in style: and she, like the figures in the Buchanan Street Tea Rooms mural, appears to be wearing a *kimono*. That he collected prints, books and objects about or from Japan can be seen from photographs of his own apartments, and his fondness for the subject was known to his friends – Hermann Muthesius gave Mackintosh Japanese wood block prints as a gift in 1900.

Although Mackintosh's study of architectural design from Japan was derived from second-hand sources – he never went to Japan himself – many

34. In Fairyland, 1897, watercolour.

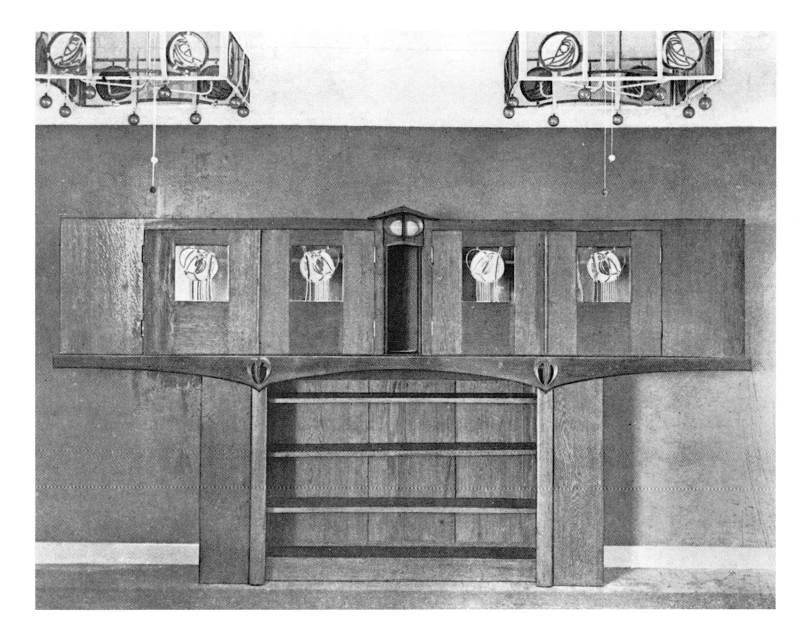

35. *Drawing-room of 'Windyhill', Kilmacolm, 1901.*

architectural details in his lexicon of motifs came from reworking and reshaping Japanese themes. For example, the crutch-like T support in traditional Japanese roofs is perhaps recalled in the rainwater-gathering boxes at the head of the downspouts on the School of Art. The circular metal "animal/shield" forms of the School's fence correspond to *kamon* or *mon*, the family crests of the Japanese. The piercing-through of planes in the furniture and timberwork recall the Oriental *sukashi* procedure, and the large cabinet called "the toy-chest" of 1901 from Windyhill undoubtedly reveals how Mackintosh could

transmute a form originating in one medium to another entirely different – a fabric kimono becomes a three-dimensional wooden construction as a piece of furniture.

The mature work: Glasgow

During the highly productive years in Glasgow, Mackintosh created much two-dimensional work and a large number of furniture pieces parallel with his architectural and interior designs. A summary of the most significant architecture and environmental work includes: Redclyffe house, 1890 (*24*); the *Glasgow Herald* building, 1895 (*22*); Queen Margaret Medical College, 1894–96 (*78*); Buchanan Street Tea Rooms, 1896–97 (*177*); Martyr's Public School, 1896 (*79*); Argyle Street Tea Rooms, 1897 (*184*); the Music Room, Craigie Hall, 1897 (*27*); designs and interior of Westdel, 1898 (*106, 107*); Queen's Cross Church, 1899 (*116*); Glasgow School of Art, 1897–99 and 1907–1909 (*P. 88*); unexecuted designs for the 1901 Glasgow International Exhibition, 1898 (*119*); the drawing-room, Dunglass Castle, 1899 the Mackintoshes' apartment at 120 Mains Street, 1900 (*122*); Ingram Street Tea Rooms, 1900; a room for the Eighth Exhibition of the Secession, Vienna, 1900 (*38*); Windyhill house, 1900–1901 (*P. 145*); a portfolio of drawings for the *Haus Eines Kunstfreundes* architectural competition, Darmstadt, 1901 (*42–50*); designs for the unexecuted An Artist's Town House and An Artist's Country Cottage, 1900 (*139–145*); the *Daily Record* building, 1900–1901 (*146*); interior of 14 Kingsborough Gardens, 1901–1902; a suite of rooms, The Rose Boudoir, at the International Exhibition of Decorative Arts, Turin, 1902 (*52*); a Music Salon for Fritz Waerndorfer, Vienna, 1902–1903 (*40*); a room exhibited in Moscow, 1902–1903; an unexecuted submission for the competition for a new Liverpool Cathedral, 1902–1903 (*117*); The Hill House, Helensburgh, 1903–1904 (*150*); The Willow Tea Rooms, 1903 (*164*); interiors for Hous' hill, Nitshill, Glasgow, 1903–1904 (*182, 183*); interior furnishings for Holy Trinity Church, Bridge of Allan, 1904; a dining room for A.S. Ball, Berlin, 1905; the Mackintoshes' house interiors, 78 Southpark Avenue, 1906 (*128–135*); Scotland Street School, 1904–1906; the Dutch Kitchen, Argyle Street Tea Rooms, 1906 (*184*); Auchenibert house, Killearn, 1906–1907; Mosside house, Kilmacolm, 1906 the Chinese Room and the Cloister Room, Ingram Street Tea Rooms, 1911 (*194*). (For commentary on the major works see pp 84–181.)

The *Glasgow Herald* building, Queen Margaret College and Martyr's Public School are all products of the Honeyman and Keppie practice, but with Mackintosh's increasingly direct and characteristic impact on the work as he was given more responsibility. The Redclyffe house, Queen's Cross Church, the School of Art, Windyhill, the *Daily Record* building, The Hill House, Scotland Street School, and the Auchenibert and Mosside houses were free-standing new buildings. All the remaining work comprises alterations, insertions and retrofitting in existing structures.

The Masterpiece: Glasgow School of Art, 1897–99, 1907–1909

"Architecture has an immense power to affect people, literally compelling them to look at it. For that reason it may be said to be the most powerful of all the arts."

Otto Wagner in *Moderne Architektur*, 1896.

The Glasgow School of Art is rightly considered Mackintosh's masterpiece. The building has been described as a foundation for modern architecture, a bold signpost pointing to the future, a spiritual, aesthetic and physical affirmation of hope and idealism. It had no precedent and no equal, but it became "an encyclopedia of possibilities" (Aldo van Eyck). Although at the time it was built it enraged and baffled the citizenry of Glasgow, even then its qualities were not completely missed. In 1900, *The Studio* described the School in this way: "The building has been designed to meet the requirements of the School and in no instance has a regard for appearance been allowed to interfere . . . Embellishments have been carefully concentrated to gain in value from

36. Glasgow School of Art, 1897–99, 1907–09, northern (facade) elevation, a composite photograph.

their juxtapositions to plain surfaces. The great windows to the north are a conspicuous feature in the elevations and the projecting roof gives sufficient light and shade to emphasize the scale. All details have been carefully worked out and the building possesses a unique character, due in some measure to the requirements and situation, but in the highest degree to the treatment of the subject by the architect." This perceptive view clearly recognizes that the building is one wherein the unimpeachable logic of the interior plan dictated the nature of the elevations.

From this logic proceeds a belief that the exterior skin is the articulation of an interior design aesthetic at work; it is not mere architectural cosmetics, but the expression of a deeply held belief. In the School of Art, Mackintosh's intentions and his originality speak clearly to us. There is a directness and an honesty that is disarming, for while it is easily demonstrable that many themes and details are derived from other sources, which he adopts and then adapts, the bold holistic mass of the building is infinitely superior to the sum of those small parts. Eliel Saarinen, the great Finnish architect, wrote on this theme: "It is fundamental

that whatever forms a man brings forth will not be altogether convincing unless they are true expressions of his life – his emotions, his thoughts, his aspirations. His art, at best, is a significant testimony of his integrity of mind and spirit, the product of his real personality. No work of art in any field can be considered a work of art unless it reveals the basic nature of the artist himself."

If we accept the wisdom of Saarinen's observations, we can see the School of Art as Mackintosh's self-portrait. It is indeed the true expression of the "significant testimony of his integrity of mind and spirit", revealing both the essential idealism and pragmatism of his character in his pursuit of perfection. His personal and professional life was conducted in some contrast to that of his contemporaries, and perhaps only in the School did Mackintosh feel that he was among a community of believers who shared his convictions and aspirations, who welcomed and respected his work. Although he demonstrated uncommon care and brilliance in the design and execution of other major works – The Hill House and The Willow Tea Rooms, for example – nothing equals the thought, creativity, intellectual diligence and pure love that he bestowed on the making of the Glasgow School of Art.

Many writers, critics and observers of his work have accused Mackintosh of an almost unhealthy obsession with perfection and detail, and of being a tyrannical Utopian. The dramatic sculptural form of much of his furniture, for example, was said to be militantly discomfiting, and he was described as an architectural egomaniac who imposed his design will at the expense of his clients. A study of the philosophic premise on which the Glasgow School of Art was designed shows that nothing could be further from the truth.

Mackintosh had graduated from the School only a few years before he created the design, and he was fully aware of the complexity and difficulty of designing space and fitments that would be appropriate and efficient, yet he made the entire building serve the requirements of its occupants. He was a man of strong convictions and an individualist, but one whose design logic deeply respected the needs of others. He believed that the artist, the architect, the designer and the craftworker were precious people, vitally important to the intellectual and cultural health of civilization and society, so Mackintosh wanted his building to be a perfect place where these special people would learn and practise their arts. The building is dedicated, in a remarkably selfless way, to serve its purpose as an institution of education through art: if there is anything obsessive or egotistical about Mackintosh's expression it is his fanatical determination to make the structure work perfectly. The entire design of the Glasgow School of Art serves the moment when pencil touches paper, paint meets canvas, chisel strikes stone.

Mackintosh was a true nationalist, but an eclectic one, though no less great for that. The eastern section of the Art School is redolent with themes of the Scottish medieval and baronial he said was so "dear to my heart", and the western section is marked by the influence of Japan, but

it is not diminished by either, and Mackintosh does nothing to conceal those references. The greatness lies in the way that he has made the building no mystery at all, yet has hidden in plain sight the magic that animates it. In many ways it is an enigmatic building, yet it is also the unambiguous embodiment of Mackintosh's philosophy. He makes the building's power emerge from what it is and what it does, rather than where it came from. It is as strong a national symbol as are the ancient standing stones of Scotland, or the chosen rocks of the gardens of Japan. The School, however, must be seen in relation to the whole range of Mackintosh's work. The School of Art building is the masterpiece which he created at the outset of his Glasgow period and it spans his professional career in the city. While some other works, like The Hill House and The Willow Tea Rooms, are fabulous concoctions of brilliance and excitement, they never equal the sombre power of the School. Without the School Mackintosh might have been characterized as "only" an extraordinary architect–designer of astonishingly seductive ability, but for having built the School he is rightly called a genius.

A tale of two cities: Glasgow and Vienna

"In 1893, The Studio first appeared in Vienna. People in England can hardly visualize what its appearance meant. It succeeded . . . in all parts of Europe . . . it was a beacon."

Amelia Levetus, Viennese correspondent of *The Studio*.

"To our master, Mackintosh, the greatest since the Gothic."

A toast at the banquet of the Kunstlerbund, Breslau, 1913.

If the publication of articles in *The Studio* brought the work of Mackintosh and "The Four" to wider attention in Britain, the same is true for middle Europe, where the influence of the work of the

Scots was both a confirmation and a challenge to the restless young Viennese architect–designers. There developed an intimate understanding of shared objectives and ideals, a brotherhood of belief between Mackintosh and three men of radical proclivity, the wealthy arts patron Fritz Waerndorfer, (1869–1939) and the architect–designers Josef Hoffmann (1870–1956) and Joseph Maria Olbrich (1867–1908). This Viennese trio were living in an aesthetic climate of rigid conservativism that, as in Glasgow, extolled the virtues of a Classical or historicist approach to the built environment, but they were increasingly attached to the progressive beliefs of Otto Wagner. Wagner (1841–1918), although respected by the tradition-bound Viennese establishment, was nevertheless at heart an innovator who supported the idealism and enthusiasm of the younger artists and architects whose activities and ideas alarmed and outraged so many in staid Vienna.

Otto Wagner was, like Newbery, his counterpart in Glasgow, a supporter and a nurturer of young talent, and his appointment as Director of the Academy in 1894 allowed his own insistent idealism to mature and enabled him to pass it on to his students. Among them were Hoffmann and Olbrich, who in 1896 entered Wagner's own architectural practice.

In 1897, the year in which Mackintosh was beginning construction of the eastern portion of the School of Art, a group of progressive young artists escaped the stifling atmosphere of the official Kunstlerhaus to create an alternative organization for the exhibition of contemporary arts, and obtained a site for the erection of a new facility, to be designed by Joseph Maria Olbrich. These artists and architect–designers who seceded from the Kunstlerhaus take the name "Secessionists", and are also known as *Die Jungen*, creators of a "Jugendstil", a "young style". They took as their motto the phrase they engraved on the pediment of Olbrich's building: "To every age,

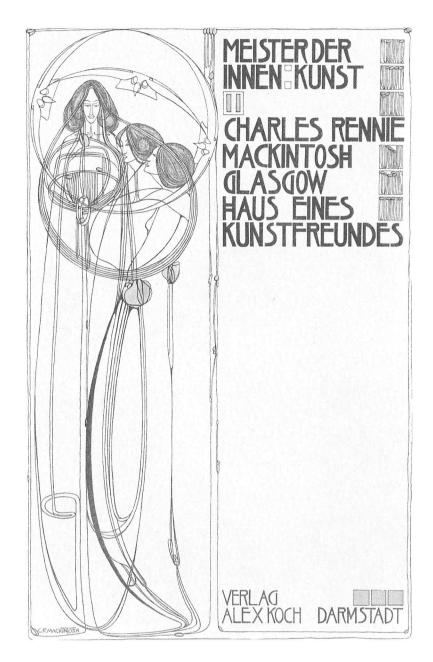

37. Frontispiece for the portfolio of colour lithographic prints, "Haus Eines Kunstfreundes" (A House for an Art Lover), Darmstadt, Germany, Alex. Koch, publisher, 1902.

its art; to art, its freedom." The painter Gustav Klimt (1862–1918) endowed the movement with a typically mystical-natural title for their new magazine, *Sacred Spring* (*Ver Sacrum*), first published in 1898. The Secession first exhibited together in 1898, while awaiting the completion of the Secession Haus later that year. Josef Hoffman and Koloman Moser (1868–1918) joined the teaching staff of the Kunstgewerbesschule

(School of Applied Arts) under its new Director, Baron Felicien von Myrbach, a Secessionist supporter, but Olbrich moved to Darmstadt under the patronage of Ernst Ludwig, the Duke of Hesse, already a patron of Ashbee and Baillie Scott, to begin to create an arts colony there at the suggestion of the ubiquitous publisher Alex Koch, who had launched *Deutsche Kunst und Dekoration*. Clearly there was abroad in the world a sense of urgency in addressing artistic issues, a restless need to make something *new*. Many of these young artists and designers began to look around for a uniting principle or shared philosophy of optimism that might unify their activities. The *zeitgeist* of the period often made the quests in different countries and cultures assume either a similar or a vastly contrary garb, which can lead to a rather pointless exercise in trying to identify who came first and who influenced whom. *Dekorative Kunst* of 1898 noted: "Evidently there are *certain things in the air* which affect our movement, in spite of all nationalism, and which are all the more easily explained in the knowledge that these things are concerned with a unifying logic and technical questions." On this matter of similarity and dissimilarity, Ashbee had written: "We may differ vitally in manner of expression in our work, in our planning, in our touch, in the way we clothe our feeling for proportion . . . but although our problems differ essentially we are together in our principles" (*Ausefuhrte Bauten und Entwurte*, 1910).

While, in Scotland, Mackintosh was receiving his practical education and dreaming of its application on his own terms, in Vienna, Wagner's teaching text, *Moderne Architektur*, of 1896 (republished in 1898) contained a philosophy that the Scots would have found naturally acceptable: a ruthless logic that necessity and function dictate form, that "truthfulness" reveals the interiors of a building through the exterior, that the "artist–builder" will create a new language for architecture which reflects nature and utilizes all the new technologies available harmoniously blended together, and that, while history was to be respected, the new world could not be a replication of "the fruits of archaeological study". The climate in Vienna was, in many ways, interchangeable with that in Glasgow, and an empathetic response was felt in the Austrian capital to the works of Mackintosh, revealed in *The Studio* (1895, 1896, 1897), in *Dekorative Kunst* and *Academy Architecture* (1898) and *Dekorative Kunst* again (1899), and until 1907 in both British and German-language publications.

Waerndorfer had visited Britain in the early 1890s and had developed an enthusiasm for the British way of life and an identification with the contemporary styles of work seen first hand in London. His library contained the works of Ruskin and Morris, and his familiarity with their ideas and the Arts and Crafts movement is reflected in his letters, which contain phrases like "honest craftsmanship"; "truth to materials"; "art for all"; and "respect" for ancient architecture and vernacular expression. Wed this to the ideals of the Vienna Secession in bringing the best of contemporary foreign art to Vienna, "not just for the sake of artists but to create a great mass of people receptive to art", and to the notion of a visual arts' "gesamtkunstwerk", and it is perhaps inevitable that there should be comments such as Josef Hoffmann's in *Der Architekt* of 1897: "It is to be hoped that some time with us too, the hour will strike when one orders the wallpaper, the ceiling painting, the furniture and utensils not from the dealer but from the artist. England is far ahead of us in this . . . we should recognize [their] interest in decorative arts and thus in art in general and we should strive to awaken it equally in us." When Waerndorfer had returned to Vienna from London, he sought to furnish his house in a style that would be freshest and newest, because "British" and "Modern", he wrote, were "at that time synonymous". He was a friend to many of the avant-garde in Vienna, collected the work of the painters Gustav Klimt, Oskar Kokoschka, Egon

Schiele, and developed an especially close relationship with Josef Hoffmann.

The Secessionist movement enjoyed a secure base of youthful support at the School of Applied Arts, where Hoffmann was appointed a Professor at the age of twenty-nine. Olbrich, also a Secessionist disciple, was to create the dramatic monumental new building for the Secession in 1898. This group of friends was so impressed with the reproductions of Mackintosh's work and Gleeson White's texts in *The Studio* that they invited the Scots designers to exhibit at the Eighth Secession Exhibition and to come to Vienna. For "The Four", this was an incredible opportunity for

recognition far from the city that seemed so heartily unenthusiastic about their works. It is not surprising that a close friendship was to develop between Hoffman, Mackintosh and Waerndorfer. The English-speaking Waerndorfer was dispatched to Scotland in 1900 to meet Mackintosh and make arrangements for the exhibition. He and his wife visited the then complete first section of the Glasgow School of Art building, saw the early Tea Rooms, the Mackintoshes' house, and the work of "The Four" and friends, went on holiday with Margaret and Charles, and formed the scotch-and-schnitzel friendship that united the two cities.

The exhibition took place late in 1900 and was

38. The Exhibition Room, Eighth Secession Exhibition, Vienna, Austria, 1900.

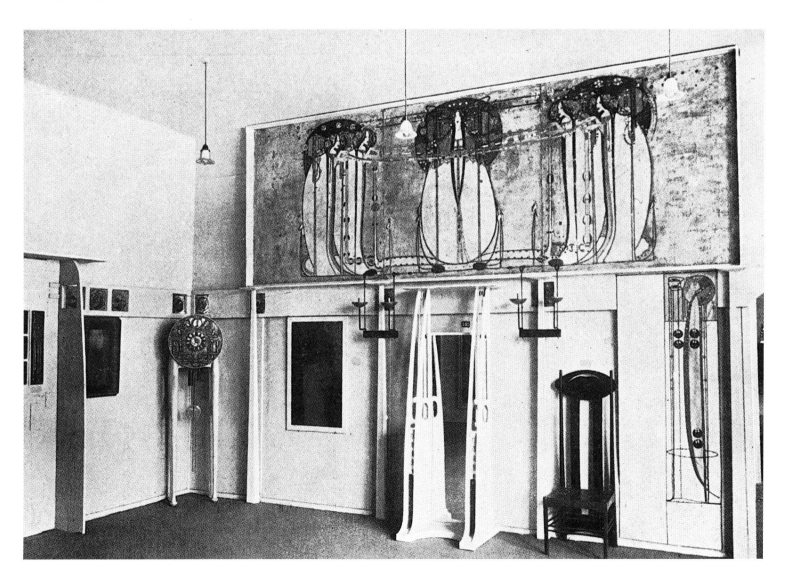

39. *The Exhibition Room, Eighth Secession Exhibition, 1900.*

considered a triumph, in terms of both critical success and work sold. The Mackintoshes were lionized throughout their visit and, if the reports are to be believed, the adoring students of von Myrbach's famous School carried them in triumph through the streets. The *Neue Freie Presse* accorded Charles the most unpronounceable honour of being "der Schottische Secessionist" and the *Neues Wiener Tagblatt* review read: "The room by Dr Mackintosh and his wife must be counted among the most striking achievements which modern art had created." The Mackintoshes' stay in Vienna, which constituted a late honeymoon (they had married a few months earlier), lasted six weeks. They were fêted throughout by their admiring hosts. Margaret made a considerable personal impact, and one newspaper described her as, "a young lady, with

reddish hair, dressed elegantly in an unusual manner [who] attracted general attention". Extant photographs of the Secession display show a room that was designed first in Glasgow, then disassembled and sent to Vienna for re-installation, and which contained items of furniture by "The Four", and a pair of large gesso murals, *The Wassail* and *The May Queen*, which were created in sections and set high on the wall filling the gap between the picture rail and the ceiling, facing each other across the room. The manner in which the site-specific furniture, the watercolours, MacNair's four-legged large clock, the lights etc., were all arranged, combined with the cool sanitary elegance of the white theme had a powerful impact in presenting Mackintosh's central idea that in an "aestheticized environment" the overall effect was most important, and that all the pieces which went to make up the interior were of secondary significance to that effect. Of all the Secessionists, it was to Hoffmann that this message spoke most directly and most seductively, for his own space at the Eighth Secession was in marked contrast with his colleagues in its simplicity and the obvious similarity of spirit it shared with Mackintosh. The sparseness and rather puritan appearance of "The Four's" room was the subject of much debate, and its influence was to be considerable: Klimt, Hoffmann, Olbrich and all the Secessionist sympathizers saw it as a confirmation of what was to be possible, and it opened a door of understanding of how, physically and psychologically, the manipulation of interior space and the integration of elements actually worked. They saw it and digested its message, but then moved forward under the power of their own ideas. From 1902 to 1903 it is fair to say that the Vienna group was no longer being influenced in any direct stylistic way by Mackintosh, though the forms they created in their parallel developments often recall each other. For example, Klimt's *Beethoven* frieze of 1902 and his installations of mosaic panels in the dining room at the Palais

Stoclet in 1906 reprise Mackintosh and Margaret's Secession installations of 1900. While they all remained deeply respectful of Mackintosh as an innovative genius and tried to have him join them in their crusade in middle Europe, they all perhaps sought to distance themselves somewhat from a stylistic similarity that could lead to accusations of slavish imitation (*The Studio* of 1900, while admiring Hoffmann's work, noted that in one interior, "the mural decorations have . . . somewhat too strong a suggestion of the familiar motifs of the Glasgow School"). At a Paris showing, Hoffmann's work was considered outstanding and, as when Mackintosh had come to Vienna, he enjoyed reviews as glowing: "It is wonderful to see how completely these Austrian artists and decorators have forgotten the past . . . how great their ardour for novelty, for freedom, from everything which might check the fancy and ambitions of the modern man in his eagerness to create a decor appropriate to the age. Chief honour in this respect belongs to Josef Hoffmann . . . he is the very soul of the new movement."

The Viennese still regarded Britain as a hotbed of innovation and experiment and were certainly aware of the work being produced there – as were the inquisitive young idealists in other countries who saw the work of the leading figures in the "English movement" and of Mackintosh in Dresden, Munich, Berlin, Turin, Moscow and Budapest between 1900 and 1906. Perhaps they agreed with the model significance of Mackintosh and the Scots, for certainly the Hungarians, well acquainted with the works of their own Odon Lechner, and those of M.H. Bailie Scott and C.R. Ashbee's Guild of Handicraft, noted in *Magyar Iparmuvgszet* in 1902: "In British decorative art, the centre of gravity has moved from London to Glasgow."

On his return from Vienna to Glasgow, Mackintosh wrote to the painter Carl Moll: "We feel very much indebted to you for the honours you and your colleages have offered us, and we will always remember with pleasure your kindness to us when we were in Vienna. I know well the artistic achievement of your exhibition. I hope that it is receiving the public recognition and support which it deserves." Margaret joined Charles in expressing the sentiment that their reception had been "the high point" of their lives. This is a chilling observation, for in terms of recognition and enthusiasm their Viennese reception was to be without equal, even though their return to Glasgow was on the eve of several major commissions (Windyhill, The Willow Tea Rooms, The Hill House, Scotland Street School, and the western extension of the School of Art), all in the period 1900–1907. Their Viennese admirers kept in touch, sent them Christmas gifts, and kept alive the deep and abiding shared belief that they would indeed together invoke the design language of the future. A 1901 edition of *Ver Sacrum* was devoted largely to the work of Margaret and Charles. Olbrich, writing to Claire Morawe in 1902, on the subject of a possible elopement due to parental disfavour, reflects the enduring admiration for Mackintosh: "It would be best if we were married in Glasgow so that we could ask dear Mackintosh to listen attentively as we affirm our vows. He is the only one who is worthy to know first that we wish to follow together the laws of Nature in her enigmatic ways."

The Viennese Hugo Henneberg bought Mackintosh's smokers' cabinet from the Secession exhibition and harmoniously united it with his own interior by Hoffmann in the latter's Artist's House on the Hohe Warte. Waerndorfer bought several small items from the Secession exhibition of 1900, but the most significant development was his commission to Mackintosh to create interiors for his Vienna home. (This was not, however, Mackintosh's first European commission: in 1898 he had made part of a dining room for H. Bruckmann in Munich, the patron likely being impelled to the commission after seeing Mackintosh's work in *The Studio*.)

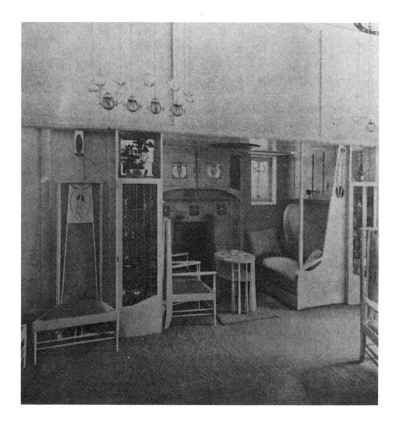

40. The Music Room, commissioned by Fritz Waerndorfer, 1902, Vienna, Austria, photographer unknown.

Waerndorfer's 1900 commission was for a music salon, a white environment of quite exceptional elegance and subtle refinement, even for the great Mackintosh: it was not installed until 1902, having been partly prefabricated in Glasgow. Hoffmann, as the most understanding and sympathetic interpreter of Mackintosh's design, assisted Waerndorfer with the installation. (Hoffmann was creating a dining room for Waerndorfer in an area adjacent to Mackintosh's *salon de soirée*.) The Music Salon contained an enormous grand piano (not installed until 1903) and exquisite panels by Margaret, based partly on her enduring fascination with Maeterlinck's *The Seven Princesses*, a story also explored by Klimt. The whole tone of the room, with the vertical stress of the high-backed chairs (almost identical to those at Mackintosh's Kingsborough Gardens home and those shown at the 1902 exhibition at Turin), yielded uncommon responses from those who were fortunate enough to have seen it: "The

composition forms an organic whole, each part fitting into the rest with the same concord as do the passages of a grand symphony; each thought resolves itself as do the chords in music till the orchestration is perfect, the effect of complete repose filling the soul" (A.S. Levetus in *The Studio*, 1912). This interior has apparently been destroyed and none of its components traced, "the most serious of the many acts of vandalism which seem to have pursued Mackintosh's work" (Roger Billcliffe).

The tragedy of Mackintosh is perhaps that he was never afforded the opportunity actually and fully to execute an unconstrained vision of his philosophy of a total integration of all the arts within architecture. The Willow Tea Rooms (1903) and The Hill House (1903–1904) are most successful, but the most intriguing expression is shown not in a real house, but in a proposal for one never built in his lifetime: *Haus eines Kunstfreundes*, a House for a Lover of the Arts, 1901. The impact of Mackintosh's designs was, therefore, neither through the publication of photographs of an extant work in the journals of the day, nor by a visit to the actual buildings, but by means of small exhibition installations and the distribution of a portfolio of full-colour lithographs which resulted from the competition that had been announced in 1900 by the publisher and interior artefacts manufacturer, Alexander Koch, in *Zeitschrift fur Innendekoration*.

The fact that Koch, influential as publisher of *Deutsche Kunst* in Olbrich's new home at Darmstadt, was the promoter of the competition ensured that it would receive great attention. Mackintosh submitted his designs for this very large project under the nom-de-plume *Der Vogel*. One of 36 entries, which included the work of Baillie Scott and Leopold Bauer, Mackintosh's entry arrived both late and incomplete and he was technically disqualified. There was no outright winner and the judges, who included Olbrich, were rather disappointed by the submissions,

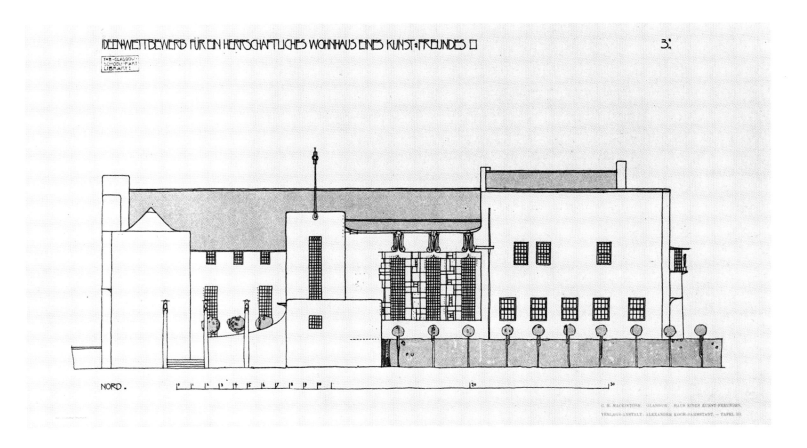

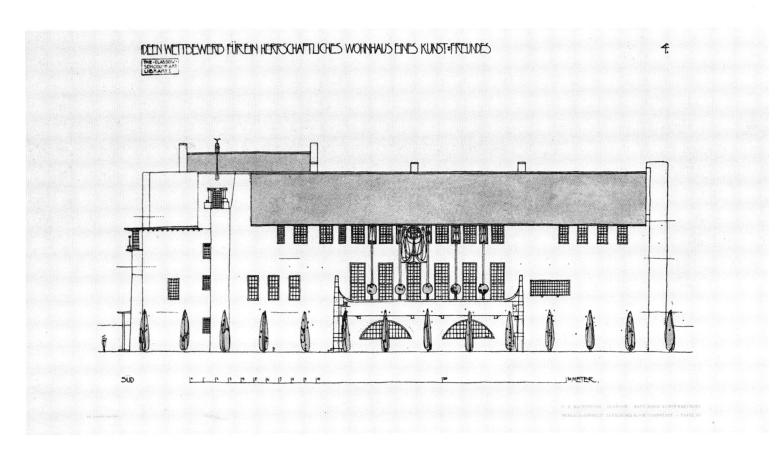

41,42. Northern and Southern elevations of "Haus Eines Kunstfreundes"
(A House for an Art Lover), from the portfolio of lithographic prints,
Darmstadt, Germany, Alex. Koch, publisher, 1902.

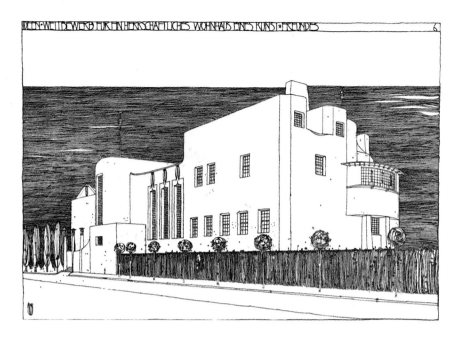

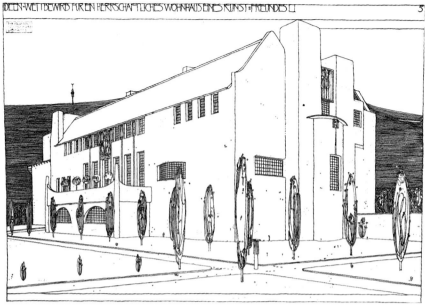

43. Drawings for Haus euies Kunstfreundes.

44. "Ideen Wettbewerb für ein Herrschafthiches Wohnhaus eines Kunstfreundes" – ideas for an aristocratic house of an art-lover."

especially those from the continent. The original competition brief had been quite specific that a visionary approach was expected: "The house is to be in the thoroughly modern style. Architects are expected to cooperate with decorative artists with modern tendencies." In their report, the judges complained, "if it had not been for the participation of foreigners, the results would have been unacceptable and questionable". In spite of their tardiness, Charles and Margaret's submission was accorded a special prize by the jury: "Among works that could not be considered owing to failure to adhere to the competition rules were designs by the nom-de-plume *Der Vogel*, which stood out because of its pronounced personal quality, its novel and austere form, and the unified configurations of interior and exterior."

The Mackintosh drawings for the Haus were published in *Deutsche Kunst*, but the real impact was the publication of the full portfolios by Koch under the title *Meister der Innenkunst* with an introduction written by Mackintosh's old friend and supporter Hermann Muthesius. (Baille Scott's and Bauer's designs were also distributed in portfolio form.) Frank Lloyd Wright's *Wasmuth*

portfolio was published in the same manner and distributed some years later, with similar effect.

The Haus design was remarkable in many respects, not least the uncompromising severity and austerity of the elevations, which rely on a drama of spareness and precision in the massing of the volumes and planes and which, as Muthesius wrote, "exhibit an original character unlike anything else known". The elevations derive from the drawings and execution of the Windyhill house of 1900, to which the Haus design bears a close relationship. For those in Vienna familiar with the architectural work of the Scot, there was an obvious reference to the south elevation of the School of Art, which was cubistic and boxy and finished in a cement render. The School had not, at this time, been published, so it is interesting to note that the Viennese were influenced not by Mackintosh's "masterpiece", the School, but by the decorative applied arts, the domestic interiors and the Tea Rooms.

A competition of this kind freed those submitting from the obvious constraints of having to work for a real client. Mackintosh's unhampered imagination allowed him to explore some unconventional themes, yet they were all consistent with his belief in designing from the inside to the outside, and the sculptural assembly of the exterior was, as in other creations, dictated by the flow and disposition of the interior functions. The logic of the planning, its progress into the elevations, the specificity of the interior designs, all were instructive lessons for the early modernists. The integration of the design work by Margaret, and the credit so clearly given to her, show how closely she and Charles could work together.

It would seem rather unlikely that the architect–designers of central Europe had been waiting with bated breath for this New Testament to appear, or had pounced on Mackintosh's Haus as the Revelation, but it nevertheless provoked

46. The Dining Room. Colour lithograph from 'Haus' portfolio, 1902.

45. The Nursery. Colour lithograph from 'Haus' portfolio, 1902.

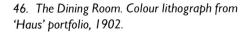

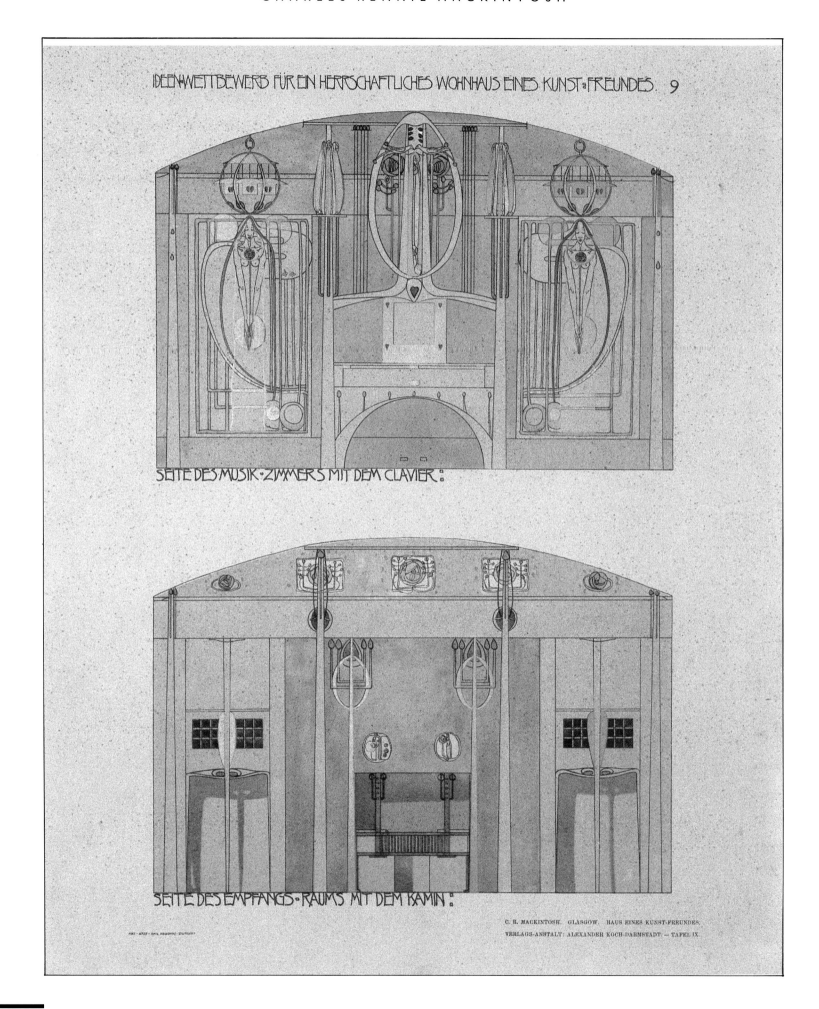

IDEEN-WETTBEWERB FÜR EIN HERRSCHAFTLICHES WOHNHAUS EINES KUNST-FREUNDES. 9

SEITE DES MUSIK-ZIMMERS MIT DEM CLAVIER.

SEITE DES EMPFANGS-RAUMS MIT DEM KAMIN.

C. R. MACKINTOSH. GLASGOW. HAUS EINES KUNST-FREUNDES.
VERLAGS-ANSTALT: ALEXANDER KOCH-DARMSTADT. — TAFEL IX.

48. *The Music Room. Colour lithograph from 'Haus' portfolio, 1902.*

49. *The Music Room for the "Haus Eines Kunstfreundes", architectural model.*

considerable discussion. The response on the Continent to the Haus portfolio was certainly mixed, but nevertheless attentive in that it provoked examination and discourse: but it was comprehensively damned by the conservative British, who sought to keep such "pernicious" influences from "infecting" stylistic developments at home. In 1902, *Our Homes and how to Beautify Them* published a reproduction of the dining-room for the Haus and reviewed it thus: "The authors of these dreadful designs, lacking artistic inventiveness, have been driven to seek originality in fantastic forms remote from any connection with Art . . . the Aesthetic Movement in its maddest moment was never half so mad as this." The Glasgow–Vienna style was, for that author, not to be recommended as a means of beautification in the British home, nor was any "foreign" influence welcomed, whether it was called the Glasgow Style, L'Art Nouveau or Jugendstil.

If Mackintosh and the Haus had any visible, direct influence it was on Hoffmann, whose

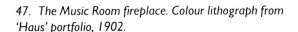

47. *The Music Room fireplace. Colour lithograph from 'Haus' portfolio, 1902.*

Sanitorium Purkesdorf of 1904–1905 bears a direct relationship in plan and mass to Mackintosh's School of Art, and it is revealed in the fabulous commission to Hoffmann to create in Brussels the Palais Stoclet mansion of 1905–1911, in which all the lessons of the Glasgow connection, the harmonic integration of architecture with interiors that were "total design" statements, were demonstrated with a flourish for a client with an unlimited budget: the Palais Stoclet is the finest creation that Mackintosh never built.

In 1903, Waerndorfer and his mother acted as financial backers for a project initiated by Josef Hoffmann; the creation of a workshop company of artisans who would create everything from houses to furniture to textiles to fashion to bookbinding, etc., which would both accept commissions and also retail directly from shops of their own design: the Wiener Werkstatte. Their idealism and enthusiasm is recalled in the Belgian architect Henry Van der Velde's comment, "the artist should no longer simply paint pictures, but rather create whole rooms and whole dwellings". (He had also shown with the Secessionists in 1900.) Such idealism was in accord with the views of William Morris that art should range widely

50. Design for the Hall. Watercolour and pencil,
from 'Haus' portfolio, 1902.

across society, not be restricted to its traditional elitist definition. In 1886 Morris had written in *The Aims of Art*: "I must ask you to extend the word Art beyond those matters which are consciously works of art, to take in not only painting and sculpture and architecture, but the shapes and colours of all household goods . . . and to extend it to the aspect of all the externals of life."

Although they had visited Ashbee's Guild and School of Handicraft in London, it was to Mackintosh that the Viennese turned for benediction in personal discussions in 1902, when both Hoffmann and von Myrbach visited him in Glasgow. Given the randomness of Mackintosh's commissioned work and his reliance on tradesmen, craftsmen and builders of varying

abilities, the idea of a coherently structured workshop of artisans committed to high quality of production must have made him both excited and envious.

The Werkstatte was not a new, startling or original idea, but the breadth of its possibilities and the remarkable financial security guaranteed by the textile-manufacturing family fortune of Fritz Waerndorfer made the enterprise rather exceptional. A number of guilds or workshops had come into existence since the 1860s, often as part of the ethic of the Craft Revival movements, often in dogmatic idealistic opposition to the effect of mechanized manufacturing processes. William Morris had formed his own company to combat the dehumanization implicit in machine production: the "poetic upholsterer" (as he described himself) had put up the money to found "The Firm" of Morris, Marshall, Faulkner and Co. in 1861 as an artisans' cooperative fomenting revolution in a new approach to architecture, design and handicrafts. A.H. Mackmurdo (1851–1942) had founded the Century Guild in 1882; Lethaby was deeply involved in the Art Workers' Guild in 1884; both the Arts and Crafts Society and Ashbee's Guild and School of Handicraft were formed in 1888. Later, the Deutscher Werkbund (1907), aided by Hermann Muthesius in Germany, was to look back on all these historic developments as well as the new Wiener Werkstatte, as did the founders of the logical coalescence of all these ideas and ideals, the Bauhaus.

The "arbeitsprogramme" (the work schedule) of the Werkstatte stated: "The work of the craftsman will be judged by the same standard as that of the painter and the sculptor . . . The unbounded evil that mass production . . . has inflicted upon the field of applied art is sweeping the whole world . . . and we have lost contact with the culture of our forefathers. We have set up our workshop. It shall be our resting point on natural soil, amid the cheerful noise of handicraft, and we shall welcome those who embrace Ruskin and Morris. We wish to establish a close contact between the public, designer and artisan and produce good simple household goods . . . our first consideration is function, usability is our primary stipulation, good proportions and correct treatment of material will be our strong points . . . As long as our cities, our houses, our rooms, our cupboards, our utensils, our jewellery, as long as our speech and sentiments fail to express in an elegant, beautiful and simple fashion, the spirit of our own times, we will continue to be immeasurably far behind our forefathers . . . " Would Mackintosh bless the enterprising venture? Naturally. In a letter to Josef Hoffmann, Mackintosh summarizes part of his most deeply

held creed: "I have the greatest possible sympathy for your idea and consider it absolutely brilliant. If one wants to achieve artistic success with your programme . . . every object which you pass from your hand must carry an outspoken mark of individuality, beauty, and the most exact execution. From the outset, your aim must be that every object which you produce is made for a certain purpose and place . . . The greatest work that can be achieved in this century you can achieve: the production of objects of use in magnificent form and at such a price that they lie within the buying range of the poorest. The plan which you and Hoffmann and Moser have designed is great and splendidly thought out . . . Begin today! If I were in Vienna, I would assist you with a great strong shovel!"

The references to "good simple household goods" that "lie within the buying range of the poorest" are, in truth, lip-service to Morris' idealism, for the Werkstatte was so notorious for the costliness of its products that even the wealthy Waerndorfer complained about the prices. Ashbee's acid comments on the elitism that accompanied such laudable ideals, and the inherent contradictions of making works "for the poorest" that in fact could only be afforded by the very wealthiest were undoubtedly shared by many: "of a great social movement [there is now] a narrow and tiresome aristocracy working with high skill for the very rich". William Morris had also been sharply aware of the same contradictions between the ideals of his own "Firm" and the reality of production costs – in 1874 he had bitterly told Sir Lowther Bell of his anger at spending his life "ministering to the swinish luxury of the rich". Although united in a dismayed reaction to increasing mechanization, the views of Morris and Ashbee were in opposition to one of the titans of modern architecture, Frank Lloyd Wright. Visiting the architect in Chicago, Ashbee had been confronted with Wright "throwing down the gauntlet" in characteristic Chicagoan manner:

"My God is Machinery, and the art of the future will be the expression of the individual artist through the thousand powers of the machine."

There was a strong underlying spirituality and a belief that the artists' creations could indeed improve the well-being of both individuals and society; Mackintosh and Hoffmann shared that vision, though the execution was another matter. It may sound quaint and amusing to us now, decades removed from the period, but when Voysey wrote, "I am an unattractive person, but if I am not graceful and comely at least I can have a graceful and comely umbrella, in order to keep up my interest in those fine qualities. Remember that cold vegetables are less harmful than ugly dishes. One affects the *body*, while the other affects the *soul*", he meant it literally, seriously and with absolute sincerity. So did Margaret Mackintosh: "The design of a pepper pot is as important . . . as the conception of a cathedral."

"Fra" Newbery remained a major force in the Glasgow art world and it was to him that an invitation came from the Organizing Committee of the International Exhibition of Modern Decorative Art, to be held in Turin, Italy, in 1902, which he intended to use as a showcase for the home-grown Scottish talent of his School, with Margaret and Charles creating a dramatic entrance tableau for the salons assigned to the Scots. Mackintosh subdivided the unsympathetic space in a simple but effective manner, making the first of the three salons his own space. In it was shown "The Rose Boudoir", a silver, pink and white space containing furniture made specifically (with rose-pattern stencilling on the canvas backs), gesso panels, "The White Rose and the Red Rose" and "The Heart of the Rose", by Margaret, and a mixture of chairs, tables, china, lamps and vases as part of the ensemble, the whole entered through a "doorway" of fabric columns with stencilled female figures and flowers "made on the spot, with paper stencils that they cut out there and then. There is nothing unusual about this, they were all trained

in the School to be very self-sufficient and turned their hands to solve any problem." (Mary Newbery Sturrock.) These tall banners continued through the space, acting as "columns" that became the demarcating "doorways" to the three Glasgow display spaces. Did Mackintosh recall, in the huge figures acting as guardians, Lethaby's comment that "every portal must have its guardians", or replay his fondness for the Japanese arts, creating *hashira-e* (pillar-banners) uniquely his own? The exhibit was a critical success, though the exaggerated responses, pro and con, that accompanied all Mackintosh's work were also evident in Turin. Some of the works were sold, others returned to Glasgow, and the venture was not considered a financial triumph. Mackintosh had travelled to Turin with Newbery and they met up with Olbrich and Waerndorfer, who bought and had shipped back to Vienna one of the most powerful and elaborate of a series of writing desks that Mackintosh designed. Newbery had evidently suggested to Mackintosh that some floral decor would be appropriate in the Rose Boudoir, to which Charles replied, "No flowers except my flowers", and they went into the countryside to gather branches and twigs so that Charles could create a suitable arrangement in the Japoniste manner.

Deutsche Kunst, The Studio and other periodicals gave extensive illustrated coverage to the exhibition. Mackintosh, busy with Glasgow commissions, was not lured from Scotland to either Vienna or Darmstadt during the "long conversations" with Fritz Waerndorfer, the Grand Duke and Olbrich, though their invitations were to be repeated until 1914, the year in which Mackintosh left Glasgow, the Werkstatte was on the verge of bankruptcy and Fritz Waerndorfer left Vienna to become Fred Warndorfer, a farmer in America.

51. Entrance to the Scottish section of the International Exhibition of Modern Decorative Art, Turin, Italy, 1902, showing stencilled banners.

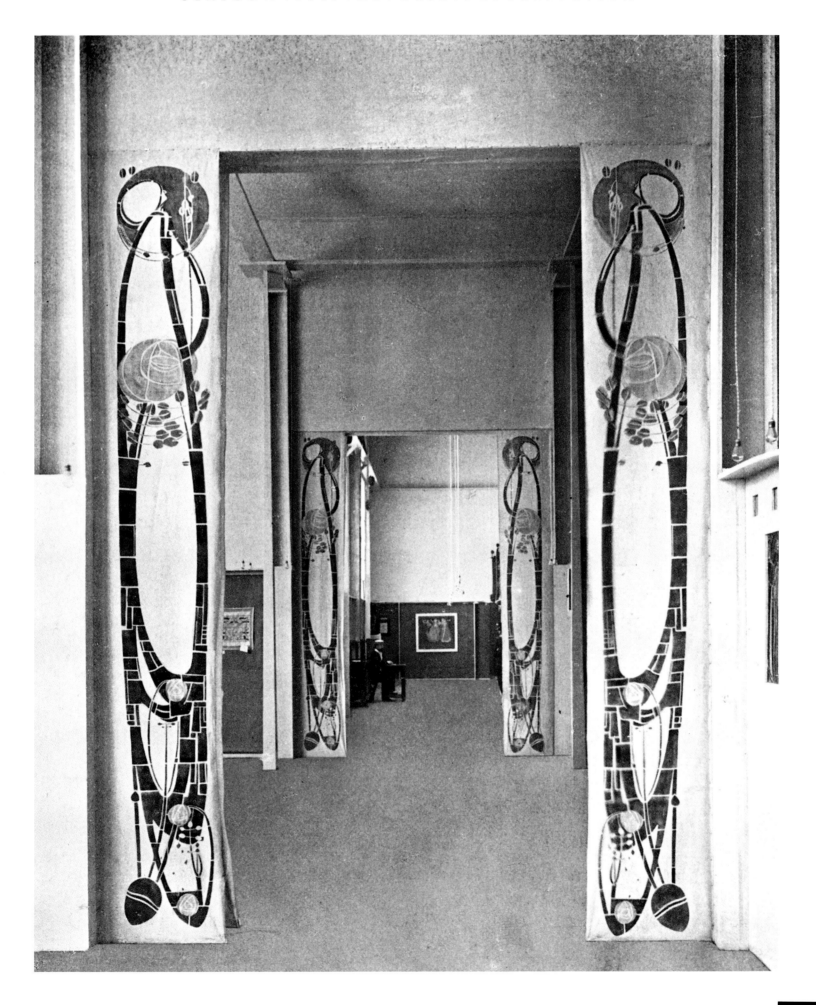

52. 'The Rose Boudoir', Mackintosh's environment at the Turin exhibition, 1902.

Olbrich and Mackintosh seemed to have had as close a brotherly relationship as Charles had with Josef Hoffmann: their friendship could have matured more deeply had Olbrich not been called to Darmstadt to found the art–design–architecture colony there. He met Mackintosh again in 1902 at the Turin exhibition. In a letter to his wife Clare he wrote, "In the evening, I got together with Mackintosh and Walter Crane for a fine meal . . . and were joined at our table by the Grand Duke and we talked until late", yet he seemed disappointed by Mackintosh's presentation: "My three rooms were the best in the show. Mackintosh also exhibited very well, but

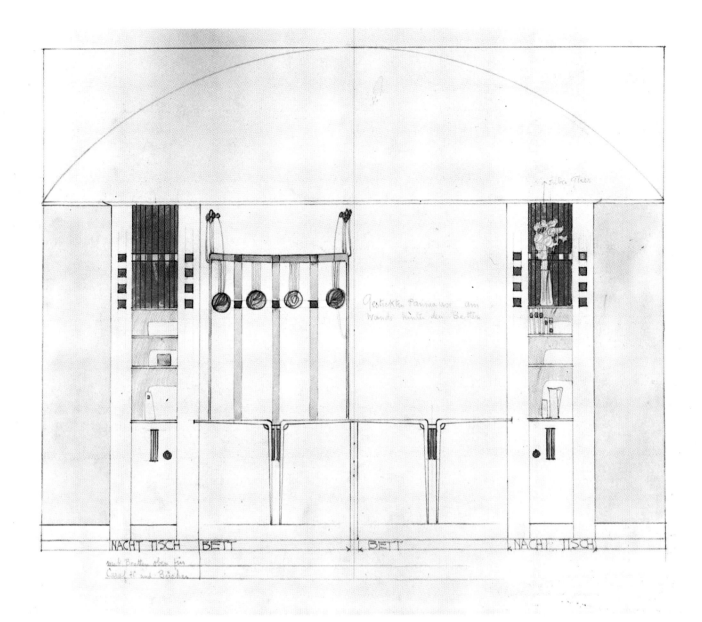

53. Design for bedroom furniture for A.S. Ball, Dresdener Werkstatten, Dresden, Germany, 1903.

his was, alas, not a fully formed interior." This Rose Boudoir, the "unformed" interior, struck the critic Ahlers-Hestermann (in the recollections entitled *Stilwende*) as follows: "Here were found the strangest mixture of puritanically severe functional forms and stylized sublimations of the practical . . . these rooms are like dreams: everywhere there are small panels, grey silks, the slenderest shafts of wood . . . here were mysticism and aestheticism,

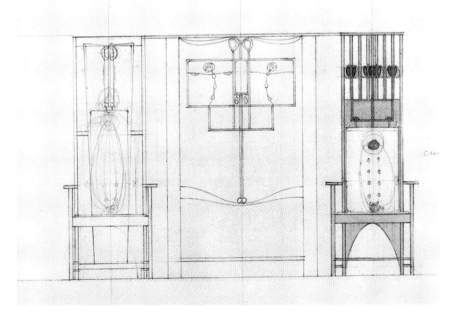

54. Furniture designs for the Turin exhibition, 1902.

and a feel of well-cared-for hands, and of delicate sensuality . . . There was scarcely anything in these rooms except two upright chairs, with backs as tall as a man, which stood on a white carpet looking at each other over a slender table silently, like ghosts." At the Moscow exhibition (not attended by Mackintosh) of 1903, where Charles' work was shown alongside that of Shektel, whom he had met in Glasgow, where the Russian had created small buildings for the 1901 international exhibition, Olbrich wrote to his wife proudly that he had sprung to Mackintosh's defence: "Today a journalist came to interview me but he was so stupid I sent him away. This foolish Russian critic allowed himself – in my presence! – to make fun of the work of Mackintosh."

Though his devotion to Mackintosh cooled, for undisclosed personal reasons, his respect for the Scot's achievements remained. What a contrast between the lonely and obscure death of Mackintosh in London in 1928, and the funeral of Olbrich, who died prematurely of leukaemia in 1908 at the age of forty, and whose obituary read: "Modern Art has suffered a grievous loss, especially here in Darmstadt and in Vienna – for he was always a Viennese and had the colourful lively fantasy, the innate elegance and ingratiating amiability of Schubert and Strauss." Postcards were sold at Olbrich's funeral, so important was he considered, and at the service trumpeters played a farewell from the top of his Wedding Tower building, while nine black-robed Muses, carrying golden laurel wreaths, descended the stairs, and an orchestra played *Gotterdämmerung*.

After the 1902 meetings between Mackintosh and his continental friends in both Glasgow and Turin came a gradual loosening of the bonds, though they kept in touch. Articles in *Deutsche Kunst, Dekorative Kunst* and *The Studio* in 1902 showed the Windyhill House in full, the 34 Kingsborough Gardens interiors, the bedroom for Westdel, drawings for the Artist's Town and Country Houses, and the stands at the Glasgow

Exhibition and the Turin exhibition. Between 1903 and 1906 *The Studio*, the German and Austrian magazines and *Academy Architecture* showed the Ingram Street fireplace, Margaret's gesso panels, beaten metalwork and embroidery, The Hill House, The Willow Tea Rooms, the Argyle Street Tea Rooms, and Scotland Street School, but after 1906 the only major publication to present Mackintosh's work was the 1907 Year Book of *The Studio*, which showed The Hill House in part, and Miss Cranston's residence Hous'hill.

Following the important continental forays of 1900–1902, Mackintosh continued to exhibit abroad, though in a limited way, nothing equalling the Vienna or Turin tableaux: in Moscow, 1903 (illustrated in *Mir Iskusstva* alongside Shektel); Dresden, 1904; Berlin, 1905; and again in Vienna at the Kunstschau in 1909. He was probably visited by Eliel Saarinen when the Finnish architect went to Scotland in 1904, he seems never to have met Frank Lloyd Wright during the American's visit, his only European journey in the period (Portugal, 1908) seems to have simply been a holiday and he seems not to have met Waerndorfer and Klimt when they were in London to show Werkstatte designs at the Royal Austrian Exhibition in 1906. The last personal contact with Vienna was probably his meeting with the Werkstatte designer Eduard Wimmer in Glasgow around 1909, when the latter was in the process of arranging an exhibition. Wimmer certainly saw the west wing of the School of Art as it was being completed and was the house-guest of the Newberys. (All the other major Mackintosh projects had been completed by this time.) Wimmer found a Mackintosh much changed from the lion of the north who had come to Vienna nine years before, for he reported sadly to Josef Hoffmann his confirmation of the rumours of Mackintosh's excessive fondness for drink.

Charles and Margaret

"I have become acquainted with one distinguished lady in my whole life – Mrs Mackintosh."

Fritz Waerndorfer

"You must remember that in all my architectural efforts you have been half if not three-quarters of them"

Mackintosh to Margaret in 1927

There has been considerable speculation on the exact nature of the relationship between Charles and Margaret, in terms of both their personal and professional lives together. It is no cliché to say that

they were soul-mates – this was attested to by many contemporary observers – but they had a natural reticence, dignity and sense of privacy that effectively prevented intrusion, so much is hidden from us. Charles exhibited a deep devotion to Margaret, and his absolute loyalty to her is demonstrated in many ways, though few would wholeheartedly support his own comment that "Margaret has genius, I have only talent." She was a natural romantic inclined toward mystic fantasy – her lifelong interest in symbolism and in the writings of Rosetti, Maurice Maeterlinck and William Morris (*The Defence of Guinevere*), was noted by her friends. Her work was always oriented toward the mysterious, but it was well-

55. Charles Rennie Mackintosh
with Hamish Davidson at 'Gladsmuir', Kilmacolm, 1898.

56. Margaret Macdonald Mackintosh, c.1905.

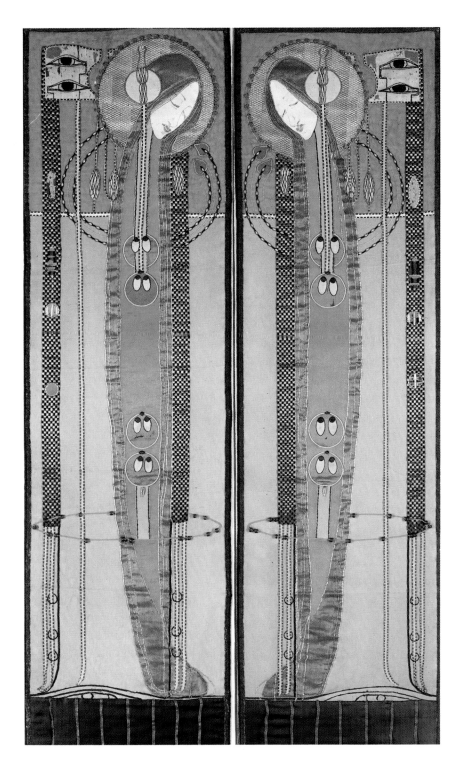

57. *Pair of embroidered panels by Margaret Macdonald Mackintosh, 1902. Exhibited at the Turin exhibition, 1902.*

crafted, inventive and intriguing, and quintessentially of the Glasgow style, replaying romantic, nostalgic, stylized visions of an imagined rather than botanically correct nature. Though she unquestionably had the ability to draw objectively, unlike Charles she seems not to have used natural forms, either flora or figuration, in a depicted

reality: they were used only as a basis for her more fantastical works.

Charles integrated her painting and metal panels into a number of the architectural ensembles that he created — the most effective and dramatic union was perhaps the Vienna Secession exhibition of 1900 — and always gave her ample credit for the embellishments she brought to the total effect, though he was always in complete control of that effect: "She collaborated with Mackintosh only in so far as he used some of her [work] . . . but I do not believe that they ever worked *together* on any design of any piece or room. He led the way and involved her only through the use of her work" (Pamela Robertson). She did, however, collaborate so closely with her sister Frances (until the MacNairs moved to Liverpool in 1899) that it is easy to confuse the work of the two — something they said was carelessly acceptable to them.

It is perhaps inevitable, given both the similarities and contrasts of their interests, that Margaret is accused of having adversely affected the development of Charles' work in the first few years of their marriage and of being a distracting and weakening influence. From about 1904 Mackintosh grew away from the Glasgow style as his own architectural vocabulary developed and, in consequence, used Margaret's work less and less. Their collaboration in the production of the interior designs for the Haus portfolio in 1901 may well be the only time when they were closely involved in creating something "together". Margaret's work was deliberately involved in the Mackintosh interior at his behest and, given his iron resolution, it is impossible to believe that he did not equally actively desire her involvement. Margaret was always an artist, but Charles had to be both an artist and an engineer who had to actually build and who therefore had a direct responsibility to clients for his architectural work. This was a burden Margaret never had to bear. While this might imply that she was less worldly and rather unrealistic, she never deserved P. Morten Shand's brutal dismissal of her entire life in 1935: "Only when he had to build, and so work in single harness, does he seem to have seen beyond that narrower orbit of his own vision which was his wife's. It would appear to have been the florid coarseness of her wholly inferior decorative talent and a firm insistence on 'me too' that too often led him into an uxorious ornamental vulgarity."

Margaret's output of work as an artist was not large, and compared with the prolific amount of her husband's it seems minute, inevitably casting her into his shadow. It would be mistaken, however, to consider her importance in relation to her production, for she was considered to be an artist of some influence and was recognized for the strange power of her work, which had a quite

58. *Detail of the lock escutcheon panels probably by Margaret Macdonald Mackintosh on a writing desk of 1900.*

Beaten brass panels with silvered plating.

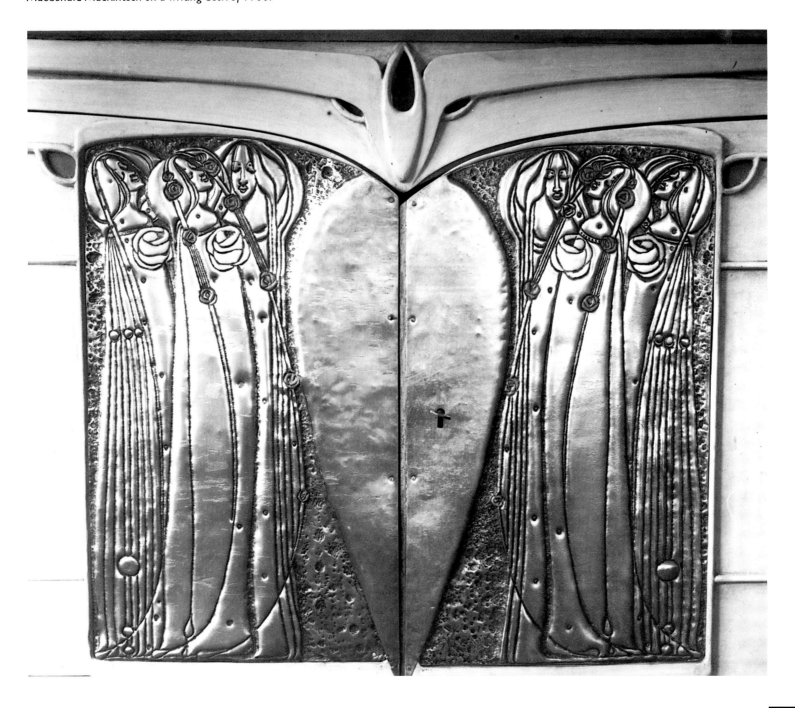

definite identity of its own before any of the collaborative projects with Mackintosh had begun. It is fair to say, however, that the strongest of her works are those in gesso, silver, metals and embroidered fabrics which she produced in association with Charles until about 1909. After that date she produced very little work, though her watercolour *La Mort Parfumée* of 1921 (considered a bereavement testimonial to her sister) and the striking 1911 menu for Miss Cranston's The White Cockade Tea Room are strong exceptions. In 1905 *Dekorative Kunst* said of her: "Mrs Mackintosh is outstanding for her illustrations of mystic poetry. Maeterlinck's imaginative writing and the visions of Rosetti echo profoundly in her soul, and under their influence her hand creates drawings, paintings and reliefs whose unusually meticulous and delicate execution never hampers their spiritual clarity."

A contemporary who knew the Mackintoshes unusually well observed: "Mackintosh was an architect first and foremost, his line was our architects' line. When they say that Margaret was such an influence on him, well, it's just not true. She did all those wiffly watercolours; how could she have influenced somebody who thought structurally and in thin hard lines? She liked Toorop, Beardsley, Rosetti, and she painted fairytales, even when she was older. She should have known better perhaps. But she was a terrific person, they both were. Very clean, very hardworking, very fastidious. She made her work in the studio in the house [78 Northpark Terrace] and was very neat, never spilled a drop, and wore white cotton gloves because she would get rashes from the turpentine – it was an allergy, I think. She was Mackintosh's complete and splendid support, he couldn't have had a better wife, she gave him a beautiful clean and peaceful house and he was completely sympathetic with her work, so he really did like to have those decorative paintings in the houses he designed." (Mary Newbery Sturrock.)

After Glasgow

The Mackintoshes left Glasgow in 1914, the year that saw the beginning of the First World War, and never returned to the city. Before they decamped, their life had been bleak, unrewarding and marked by Charles' general ill-health, lack of concentration on his work, a sharp loss of self-confidence and heavy drinking.

Unlike his middle European counterparts (Wagner, Olbrich, Hoffmann), Mackintosh had never taught. When he left Glasgow, he left behind no "school" of architecture or design. All his creative talent had been expressed either in his own private studio or in the offices of the architectural practice.

The situation at the offices of Honeyman and Keppie was said to have been electric with tension, clients complaining about Mackintosh's behaviour, absences from the office and carelessness in overseeing projects. Never well-disposed toward his fellow practitioners in Glasgow, he had few friends and fewer supporters. Neither Kate Cranston nor Newbery (who was himself then so debilitated by a nervous illness that he left the School and was too incapacitated ever to return), Davidson nor Blackie, had any work for him, and relations between Mackintosh and Keppie, equal partners in the firm, progressively deteriorated. The point must be made, however, that the economic situation in Glasgow in that year of the War had adversely affected other firms, and some had "gone to the wall". Keppie's falling income cannot be entirely blamed on the misbehaviour of his previously productive partner, but between 1911 and 1913 the firm began to drift perilously close to disaster. The accounts show that during these years the usually substantial profits had fallen to under 250 pounds and then to less than 80 pounds. Although there are apocryphal stores of flaming rows between the two partners (Honeyman had retired in 1900) the evidence is that Keppie retained his respect for the unrepentant renegade he had taken into his office years before. He was courteous, though chilly, in his letters to Mackintosh, and scrupulous in ensuring that Mackintosh received every penny of funds entitled to him from the settlement of the mutual agreement to dissolve the partnership. However, in a reported conversation overheard in 1933, Jessie Keppie is said to have scolded her brother for having "sacked" Mackintosh.

Charles and Margaret quietly slipped out of the city and departed to the gentle countryside and shores of the remote waterside village of Walberswick in Suffolk, England, renting accommodation next to the summer painting/ holiday home of the Newberys. Always his staunch supporter, Newbery considered it "a national calamity" that Charles has ceased to practise architecture. In Walberswick the Mackintoshes lived quietly while Charles created a beautiful series of tranquil flower studies notable for their strength of draughtsmanship and masterly control of the watercolour medium. The nature studies were for a volume to be published by a German press, but the onset of the war prevented its completion. He had returned to the pursuits of his childhood and studentship, prolific and alert to the endless source of inspiration that derived from the observation of nature. Demoralized after leaving Glasgow, the flower studies appeared to revive him, and they recall a phrase from the 1902 lecture on "Seemliness" he had given in Glasgow: " . . . flowers will often change a colourless cheerless life into an animated thoughtful thing". When they moved to England Mackintosh was forty-six, Margaret forty-eight.

As early as 1903 Mackintosh had written to Hermann Muthesius about his "feelings of despondency and despair" and his suffering "antagonism and undeserved ridicule". Before leaving Glasgow in 1914, Mackintosh had a last meeting with his Hill House patron Walter Blackie. Blackie was greatly taken aback at the wrecked condition of his friend, whom he found "in a deeply depressed state of mind . . . he spoke dolefully . . . of how hard he found it to have received no general recognition . . . that only a very few saw merit in his work and that many had passed him by." Blackie tellingly comments that after the success of The Willow an American visitor had urged Mackintosh to go to the New World where "a fortune awaited him", a suggestion he discounted because "his ambition [was] to work for his native city of Glasgow". This hope seems to have lived on in Mackintosh. In spite of his demoralized condition when he left Glasgow, he retained ownership of his house until 1919 (the MacNairs lived there for a while), perhaps harbouring some lingering hope of returning to start anew.

Attempts by the Secessionists to lure him to the Continent also failed, though during his last year in Glasgow he must have given the invitation serious thought. The war precluded any resolution of the matter.

It is not the intention of this text to review the non-architectural works of the later years; suffice it to say that, apart from the 1916 commission of 78 Derngate and various unexecuted architectural projects, Mackintosh concentrated on a series of flower and plant studies that became progressively abstract and led to a large number of exciting designs for textiles which at least reached the production prototype stage at Foxton's and at Sefton's, and eked out a living in London and the south of France where he made a series of watercolours on landscape themes before returning to London, and dying there, in 1928.

"The Chelsea Years" of 1915–23 were, however, a regenerative period for the Mackintoshes during which, despite Charles' inability to create an independent architectural practice and their somewhat limited income, they seemed to contemporary observers to be settled and happy. The war had turned the entire British economy away from the building industry to

59. The hall, 78, Derngate, Northampton, 1916.
Photographer unknown.

machinery and the technology of munitions as the "war to end all wars" dragged on for four years. During Charles' years in London he and Margaret were part of a large circle of people practising or associated with the arts and literature, including George Bernard Shaw, the composer Eugene Goosens, the graphic designer McKnight Kauffer, photographer E.O. Hoppe, critic Frank Rutter, the dancer Margaret Morris (with whom the Mackintoshes collaborated on stage design, and Charles in 1920 designed a new but unexecuted theatre building in a form that recalled the work of Olbrich in Vienna and Darmstadt), her husband, the painter J.D. Ferguson, and the artists Derwent

Wood, Paul Nash, and the notorious Welsh bohemian painter Augustus John (of whom it is said that he alcoholically corrupted Bertie MacNair during their Liverpool years together) – for whom Mackintosh may have executed a new studio interior.

While moving in London circles Charles appears to have obtained commissions for works, but none of these actually progressed to a conclusion. In London he was largely unknown and certainly found no patron to become the equal of Newbery, Cranston, Blackie or Davidson. What works were executed were so minor as to be largely irrelevant, with the notable exception of

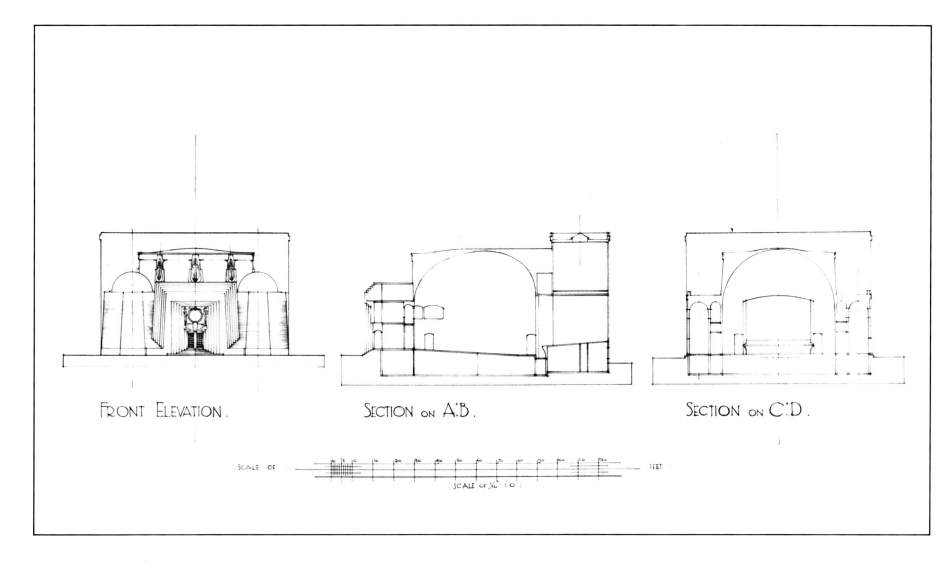

FRONT ELEVATION.   SECTION ON A-B.   SECTION ON C-D.

60. *Design for theatre for Margaret Morris, Chelsea 1920. Elevation and sections. Ink pencil and wash on cream paper.*

61. *Design for theatre for Margaret Morris, Chelsea 1920. Plans. Ink pencil and wash on cream paper.*

the powerful geometric forms of the unexecuted block of studios and apartments for the Arts Service League in Chelsea of 1920. The major achievement of the London years was the commission in 1916 of remodelling the small house of 78 Derngate, in Northampton, for the clever, informed and astute engineer Wynne Bassett-Lowke as a home for him and his new bride, Miss Jones. The interiors are an astonishing contrast to those of the Glasgow period and again demonstrate the continuous, unarrested development of Mackintosh's design vocabulary, predicting the vibrant geometry of Art Deco and the applied arts of the "Jazz Age". (Illustrations 188–192, see pp. 176–181 for commentary.)

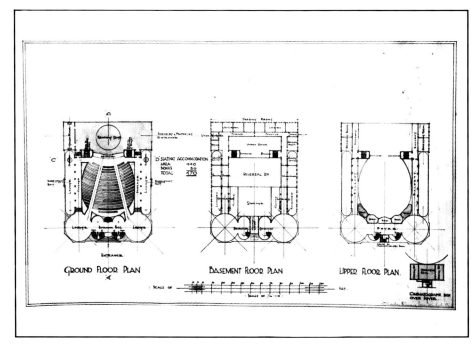

GROUND FLOOR PLAN   BASEMENT FLOOR PLAN   UPPER FLOOR PLAN.

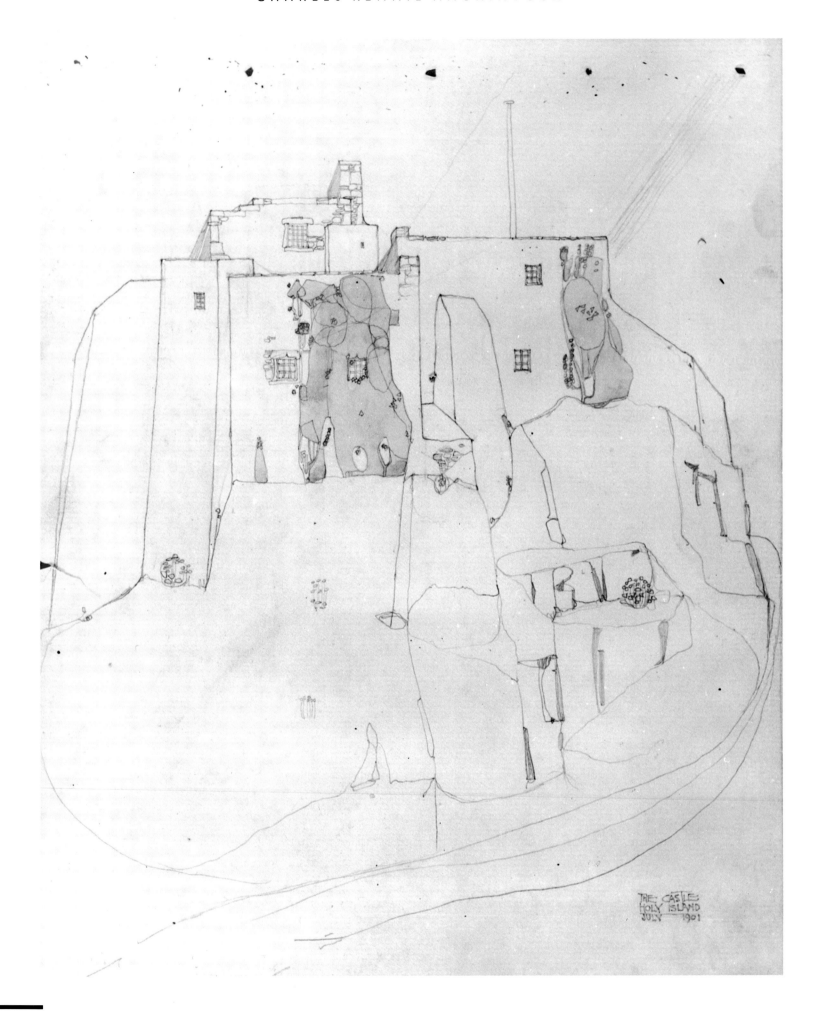

The final year

The Derngate commission of 1916 resulted in little interest and no further major opportunities. By 1919, the Mackintoshes were experiencing severe financial problems, to the extent of having to ask their old Glasgow friend, William Davidson, to buy a flower study (or even take it in pawn) to tide them over. In the same year they sold the Glasgow home. In 1923, the Mackintoshes left Britain for the Continent, not for Vienna and a reunion with his Secessionist friends, but to the warmth of Port Vendres in the south of France, where Mackintosh painted a series of magnificent watercolours in the drenching sunshine that gave such clarity and precision to the landscape. Although in both time and place he was far from his native soil and culture he bridges the gap in the powerful small painting *Le Fort Maillert* of 1927. Compare this with his 1901 drawing of Holy Island, Scotland, both depicting cubistic castles growing from the stone, proceeding by man's hand from nature.

In 1927, the year in which Charles' devoted promoter Hermann Muthesius died, the Mackintoshes returned to London from Port Vendres, Charles having suffered a serious illness diagnosed as cancer of the tongue. Confined to hospital and unable to speak, he was taught a rudimentary sign-language by Margaret Morris. In those days students in the great teaching hospitals were required to observe closely the symptoms of the patients, and it is said that in Mackintosh they found an obliging patient who allowed them to study and to draw the very cancer that was killing him: after their examination he laid out their studies on his bed and corrected them in an impromptu drawing-lesson. For Mackintosh the pursuit of perfection was a personal quest which, for him, lay in architecture and the applied arts, but it was also a quest that he respected in others. If he could help even young doctors in their search by the use of his own special talent then he would be happy to do so. He died in 1928 and was cremated at Golders Green Cemetery, in a quiet ceremony attended by a very small group of his friends. The Mackintoshes had no children. Margaret died five years later.

63. Stained glass panel, 1902.

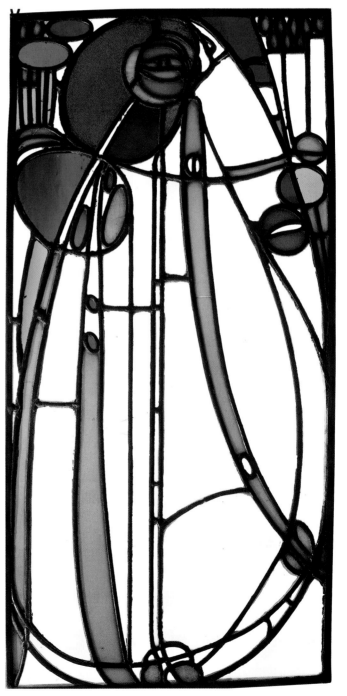

62. The Castle, Holy Island, 1901, pencil and watercolour.

"A Scoto-Continental 'new art' threatens us with its delirious fantasies, to make the movement for novelty a target for the shafts of scoffers and a motive for laughter . . . "

Our Homes and How to Beautify Them, London, 1902, describing Mackintosh's interiors for the *Haus eines Kunstfreundes*.

"First the scoffers must be overcome, and those who are influenced by the scoffers must be taught that the Modern Movement is not the silly hobby-horse of a few who will achieve fame comfortably through eccentricity, but that the Modern Movement is something living, something good, the only possible art – for all, and for the highest phase of our time."

Charles Rennie Mackintosh in a letter to Josef Hoffmann concerning the founding of the Wiener Werkstatte.

"Mackintosh holds up the banner of Beauty in the dense jungle of ugliness."

Hermann Muthesius, 1905.

"Nowhere has the Modern Movement in art been entered upon more seriously than in Glasgow, where the church, the school, the house, the restaurant, the shop, the poster, the book, have all come under the spell of the new influence . . . No artist owes less to tradition than does Charles Rennie Mackintosh: as an originator he is supreme. The critic who dismisses the new movement with a sneer has missed the charm of intention that seeks to give a rational, a soothing setting to the complex strenuousness of modern existence. If communities could be formed in ideal towns and hamlets,

founded on the best principles of the new art, the effect on individual and national health and temperament would be manifest."

J. Taylor, *The Studio*, 1906.

"His death was a loss to all the world. Not many men of his calibre are born and the pity is that when they are gone such men are irreplaceable. In my last talk with Mackintosh, I grouped him with Leonardo da Vinci . . . and in looking back I feel I may not have been far wrong. Like Leonardo, Mackintosh it seemed to me, was capable of doing anything he had a mind to."

Walter Blackie, client for The Hill House.

"If I were God I would design like Mackintosh."

Robert Mallet-Stevens to the Scots painter E.A. Taylor.

"There is hope in honest error, none in the icy perfection of the mere stylist."

Charles Rennie Mackintosh quoting J.D. Sedding.

64. Le Fort Maillert, *1927, watercolour.*

65. Wall clock for the Glasgow School of Art, 1910, various sizes, electric, controlled by a master-clock.

66. An aphorism by the architect J.D. Sedding often quoted and used as a motto by Mackintosh.

67. The signboard over the entrance doors, Glasgow School of Art.

The Mackintosh Memorial Exhibition of 1933

In May 1933, Glasgow's first major exhibition of Mackintosh's work was held at the McLellan Galleries. Amongst the exhibits were also examples of Margaret's work. The exhibition was opened by Sir Robert Rait, Principal of Glasgow University.

The following is an extract from the Glasgow Herald, May 4, 1933, reviewing the exhibition:

"The creative genius of Mackintosh found an expression not only in pure architecture but also in painting and in the design of industrial fabrics and furniture and the collections now brought together contains exhibits of extraordinary beauty and originality in all these spheres of art."

68.

"If one were to go through the lists of truly original artists, the creative minds of the modern movement, the name of Charles Rennie Mackintosh would certainly be included even amongst the few that one can count on the fingers of a single hand"

Hermann Muthesius (1861–1927)

69.

"Our designers can design in any style . . . every old method is at our finger ends . . . We are critics: we are artists. We are lovers of old work: we are learned in historical and aesthetic questions and technical rules and principles of design . . . Yet our work hangs fire. Why?"

(J.D. Sedding 1837–1892)

70.

"It is indeed a great delight to oppose an all powerful enemy, and this is precisely the reason why Charles Mackintosh is working in Glasgow."

Anonymous writer in *Dekorative Kunst* (1906)

71.

Fernando Agnoletti on the Hill House, published in
Deutsche Kunst und Dekoration, 1905

72.

"... But there is so much decorative method in his perversion
of humanity that despite all the ridicule and abuse it has
excited, it is possible to defend his treatment, for when a man
has something to say and knows how to say it the conversion
of others is usually but a question of time"

The Editor of *The Studio*, 1897

73.

"*a work of art is a successful work of art in so far as it
achieves an organisation of perceptual material into a single
organic whole from which emerges a new and unique
perceptual quality in awareness.*"

Harold Osborne *Theory of Beauty* (1852)

74.

*"In Holland, in particular, his work is held in the highest
esteem and it is said that at one meeting of Dutch architects,
at which he was not present, the only toast given was that of
'Charles Rennie Mackintosh!"*

From the *Glasow Herald*, May 4, 1933

75.

"I felt keenly that there ought to have been a central monument to Mackintosh, for he anticipated almost everything there. To this great artist some day surely justice will be done"

Mr Muirhead Bone writing about the International Exhibition of Decorative Art, 1902

Commentary
on the major works

Commentary on the major works

In the years 1890 to about 1896–97 Mackintosh's most personal expression was not in architecture, but in paintings, posters, metalwork and furniture. Most of this work was created away from his duties in the architectural offices of Honeyman and Keppie. Unconstrained by the rigours of having to abide by rigid briefs and commissions he boldly experimented in various media. There is not doubt, however, that his colleagues at the practice

were fully aware of the nature of this personal work: Mackintosh, for example, created a book-plate in his highly characteristic style as a gift to John Keppie.

At the Honeyman and Keppie practice he gradually became more involved in the commissions of the firm and made more contributions to them which were distinctively his own. The firm recognized and utilized Mackintosh's exceptional drawing skills, and the three perspectives he produced for the firm between 1893 and 1896 are notable for the clarity and strength of the line, and the monumentality he accords even to a modestly scaled building. The appearance of motifs and forms declare the ability and interests of the young architect, but one who had to work within a format determined and ruled by the firm's partners, who had the commission.

The Glasgow Herald building, designed 1893–94 (22), has a corner entrance beneath a massive tower, and while most of the design is clearly that of the practice, the hand of Mackintosh is to be seen in the relationship the tower has to his drawings and impressions of the campanile tower at Siena, which he had seen during his Italian visit two years earlier. The drawing was published in *Academy Architecture* in 1894. Queen Margaret's College, designed 1894–95, (78) demonstrates the surer sophistication of Mackintosh's hand, which is more clearly evident. Although the design is ascribed to John Keppie, there are elements of Mackintosh that appear here for the first time, and which reappear in subsequent works in an amplified manner: the plainness of the walls, the apparent randomness of the windows disposed in direct relationship to the internal functions, a strong, simple joining together of the vertical planes that recalls the Scottish tower-house form, and a plan that dictated everything – in accord with Mackintosh's belief in the logical reality that function conveys form in a continual and rational

76. The Glasgow Herald Building, detail.

77. Bookplate for John Keppie.

UNIVERSITY OF GLASGOW MEDICAL
QUEEN MARGARET COLLEGE DEPARTMENT
JOHN HONEYMAN
AND KEPPIE
ARCHITECTS

*78. Queen Margaret Medical College, 1894, perspective elevation,
pen and ink.*

flow. He planned the interior functions and purpose and let them dictate how the elevation grew in the conscious "inside-to-outside" logic he was later to apply in the School of Art building and The Hill House. The interior contained a two-storey vestibule and museum, each a prototype for enhanced execution in his next two buildings. The drawing is also noteworthy for the manner of integrating the charming contemplative figure, reading, no doubt, an "improving work", and the fanciful bushes and trees which are drawn as

though nature herself conformed to "The Glasgow Style", The perspective was published in *British Architect* early in 1896, and *Building News* described it as "an excellent structure, treated with boldness and simplicity and originality in the details".

In Martyr's Public School, (79) designed in 1895, Mackintosh's direct involvement in both planning and execution is considerably more apparent. The tall, thin windows and the sculptural decoration of the main entrance create a dramatic threshold and

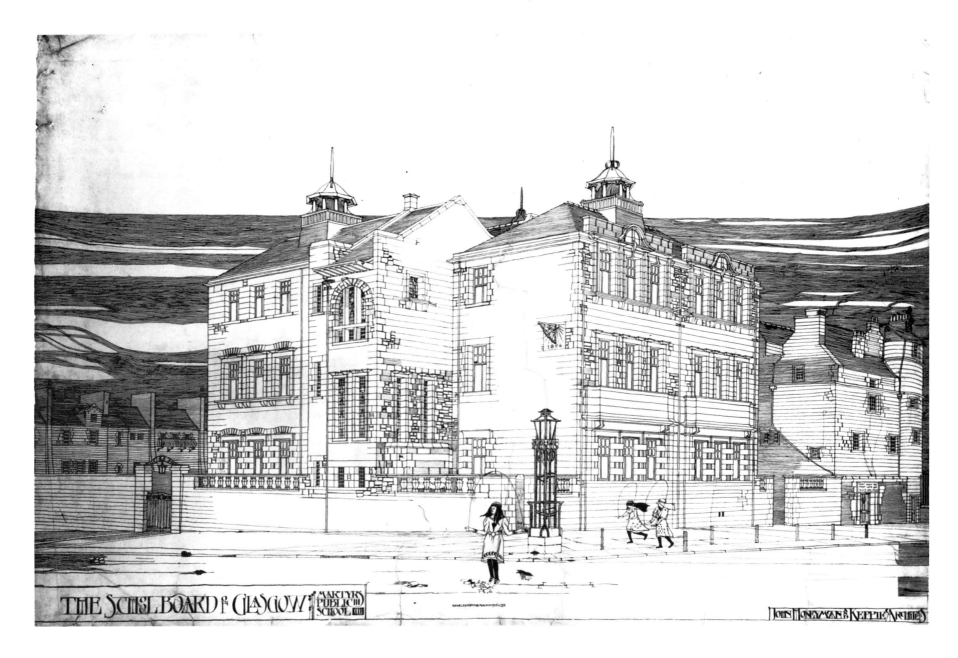

79. Martyr's Public School, 1895, perspective elevation,
pen and ink.

are, again, thematic characteristics we see replayed in later works. The interior presages the spatial sense of the Museum of the later School of Art, light streaming into the main hall of the building complex from a pitched roof of translucent glass. While the mass of the School building is the subject of the drawing, a humorous element appares in the three girls in spotted dresses skipping ropes outside the building, their Egyptian burnouses a surprisingly haut-couture accessory for Glasgow's climate. Note also the equally interesting fantasy lamp and tenement building to the right of the proposed school – it is Mackintosh's own invention, very Scots, very Baronial, certainly not a depiction of what was actually there on Parson Street (the street on which he had been born). The increasing "Toshification" of these features, like the trees in the Queen Margaret College drawing and the tenements to the right of Queen's Cross Church (as seen in his 1897 perspective), indicates Mackintosh's greater willingness to reveal the origins and models for the architecture that was to be his own. The drawing was published in *Academy Architecture* in 1896.

The Glasgow School of Art

"The north facade of the School is one of the greatest achievements of all time, comparable in scale and majesty to Michelangelo."

Robert Venturi in a letter to the author.

"Mackintosh was one of the purifiers of modern architecture."

Mies van der Rohe

In June 1896, two years aftr Mackintosh had left the School, "Fra" Newbery and the Governors of the School of Art announced a competition for the design and construction of a new building. Newbery's conviction was that the future of the thriving School could be assured only in new premises as those currently available were now hopelessly overcrowded. A combination of his high standing, determination and absolute commitment to his task virtually guaranteed the success of the undertaking. No one, however, could have guessed at the nature of that success, or that from Newbery's schedule of the School's needs – the "Conditions of Competition" – would spring one of the most daringly original and important buildings to have been erected in the then new twentieth century. It has been said, with considerable truth, that modern architecture began when Mackintosh built the Glasgow School of Art. In his design for the north facade, Mackintosh threw up a defiantly bold barrier against the tides of revivalism and historicism. The building was a declaration of faith and a clarion call to those who believed in the hopes of the future.

The site was a difficult one, a narrow strip of land running on an east–west axis atop a very steep incline (a small hill termed a "drumlin") called Garnethill, close to the heart of the city, and Newbery defined the needs of the institution quite specifically (possible even in consultation with Mackintosh), so considerable credit goes to him for his ability to describe those needs accurately. The combination of such specificity with the problems of the site led to a situation in which those architects who had been invited to enter protested that it was simply not possible to erect the required structure under such constraints. The relatively small budget of 14,000 pounds was also a serious deterrent: in booming Glasgow, where the City Chambers had been erected just a few years before at a cost of nearly a million pounds, the School of Art Competition was considered rather trifling. The Governors replied with the plaintive cry, "It is but a plain building that is required", but to little avail; and in the end compromises were reached that centred on how much could be built for the stated budget. Independent assessors in London counselled the Governors that they highly approved of one particular set of the anonymous competitors' plans. Possessed of remarkable foresight, they wrote that this building would be "better than any that could be obtained from the other designs". The winning submission was revealed in 1897 as by the firm of Honeyman and Keppie, but the authoritative and characteristic design was uniquely that of the twenty-nine-year-old Charles Rennie Mackintosh. Newbery had used his considerable influence to ensure the result of the competition, so he must have been delighted at the successful outcome, though he was not capable of coercing his Governors into agreeing to his recommendations. Mackintosh's submission (the others have never been found, so comparison is impossible) won on its various merits. Thus a combination of circumstances – the modest size of the project, the constraints of the low budget,

80. Northern and western elevations.

his junior position in the firm resulting in his being given this chance, the difficult site, Newbery's very specific list of non-negotiable requirements, the advice of the outside assessors, his friendship with Newbery – all led to Mackintosh's "masterpiece" being in effect the first building he created. However, what his design first created was controversy.

Like his jilting of Jessie Keppie, with all the social implications that surrounded such an act in

Victorian Glasgow, Mackintosh's designs for the School of Art were considered scandalous. The austerity of the building, its lack of obvious historical references, the apparent overscaling of the windows, the lack of classical references, the absence of sculptural embellishments, the asymmetrical facade and the severity of the box-like hulk caused much adverse commentary despite the inherent nobility and dignity of its powerful presence. For a society that had come

81. Glasgow School of Art, 1897–99, 1907–09, elevation to Renfrew Street (north, the facade) pen and ink with watercolour.

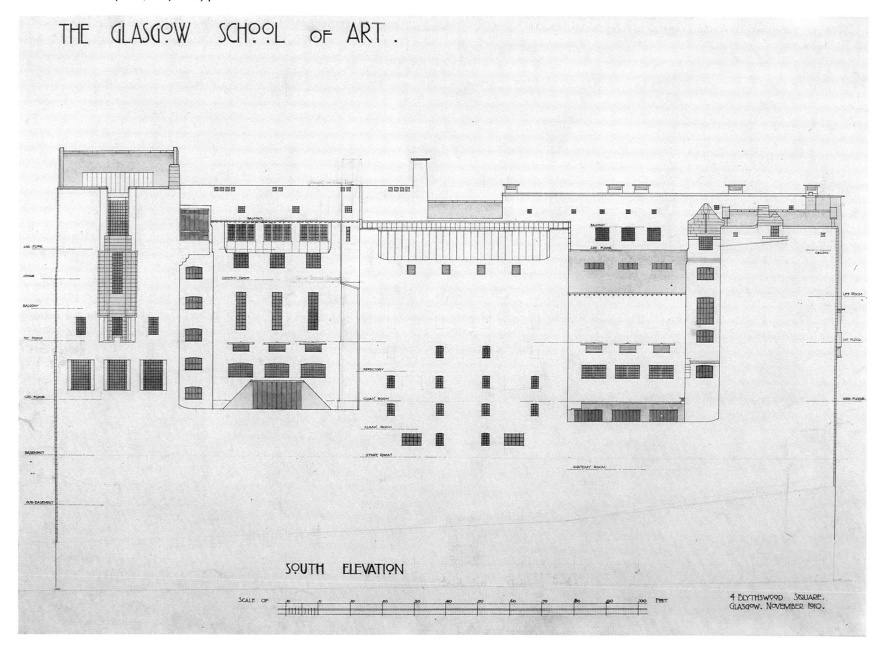

THE GLASGOW SCHOOL OF ART.

SOUTH ELEVATION

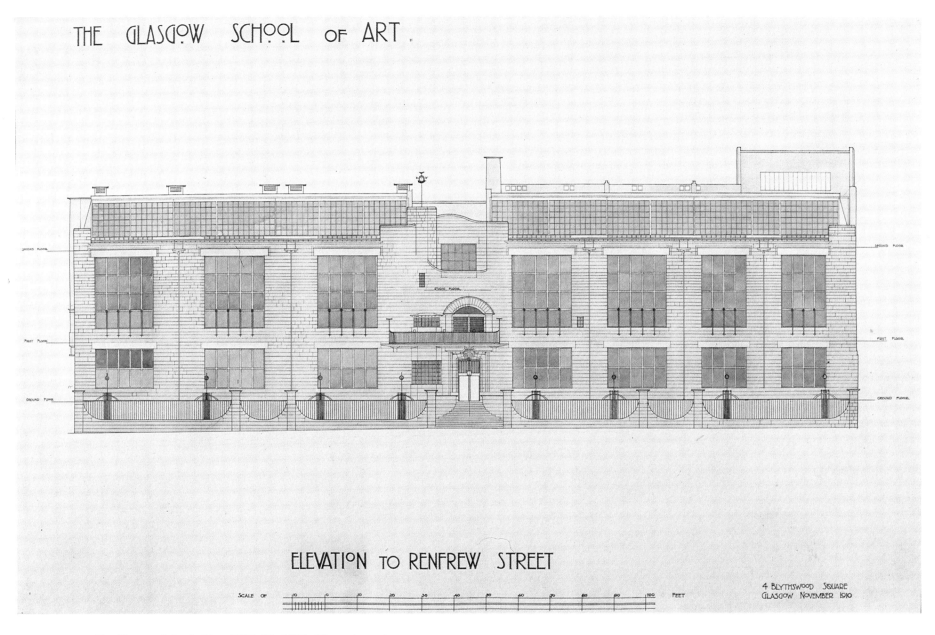

THE GLASGOW SCHOOL OF ART.

ELEVATION TO RENFREW STREET

4 BLYTHSWOOD SQUARE
GLASGOW NOVEMBER 1910

82. Glasgow School of Art, 1987–99, 1907–09, southern elevation, pen and ink and watercolour.

to accept "foreign" architectural forms as being the most seemly for a northern British city, the arrival in Glasgow of Charles' design was less foreign than it was alien. Although the building contains many reinterpreted Scottish themes deriving from his interest in the baronial-medieval past of his own country, it was as though his detractors had lost touch with that old consciousness and national identity and failed to appreciate his return to those themes. The building's odour of Continental Art Nouveau, with a suspicion of Japonisme, and its

utter "newness" served only to further damn the work. "The 'newness' of Mackintosh was the outcome of his instinct to design for practical requirements and to give these decorative expression. That being his driving impulse he could not help being 'new' in his result, however many hints and suggestions he had received from the past." (Walter Blackie, client for The Hill House.)

The building as constructed is a towering rectangular block that fills the site, stripped down, lean, with almost no decoration at all. It is austere,

91

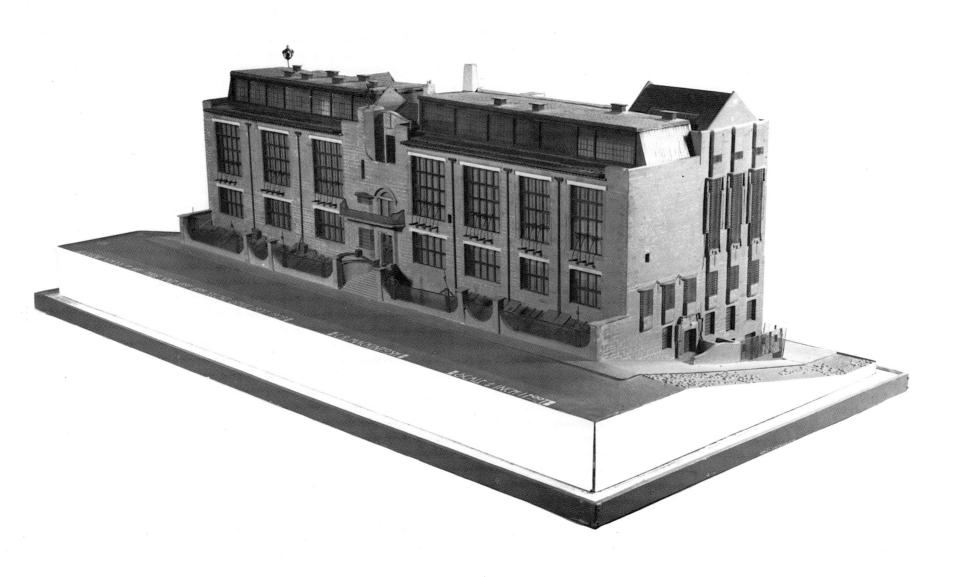

83. Glasgow School of Art, 1897–99, 1907–09, eastern elevation (1897–99 phase) and northern facade elevation, architectural model.

puritanical, fundamentalist, rational and arithmetic. For a population at home in pompous buildings encrusted with sculptures, carvings, reliefs and all manner of architectural jewellery, the School was exactly what they did not like, but it was exactly what the Governors had asked for, and what Mackintosh had supplied: "a plain building". The facade, with its huge studio windows – the proportions were defined by Newbery – in which the percentage of fenestration outweighs the stonework, was a source of astonishment. If the onlookers could accept the facade, dressed in a fine honey-straw sandstone, the back was "the limit". The northern facade faced on to an existing

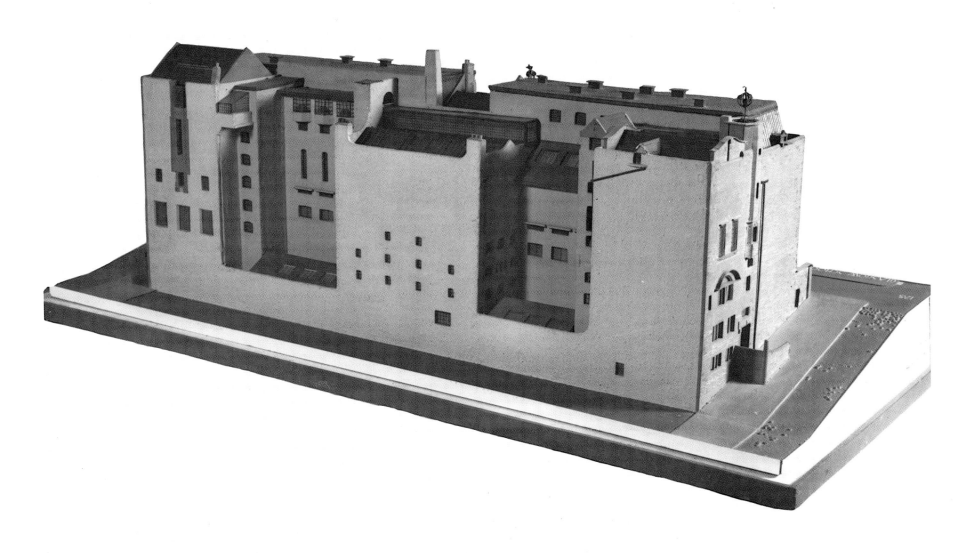

84. *Glasgow School of Art, 1897–99, 1907–09, western elevation (1907–09 phase) and northern elevation, architectural model.*

road, with buildings opposite to act as a foil in the street environment, but the southern elevation was cubistic, plain cement-rendered planes rising sheer and forbidding. A ghostly concrete castle perched on a precipice. It was this southern elevation that most people saw as it towered, like a grey monolith, over the ornate buildings on busy nearby Sauchiehall Street. It was an affront. Locally it was said that Mackintosh should have been horsewhipped for having "shown his bare arse to the face of Glasgow".

Rage and reaction often accompany the erection of new buildings offensive to many. It is no surprise to read that it was the same at the end

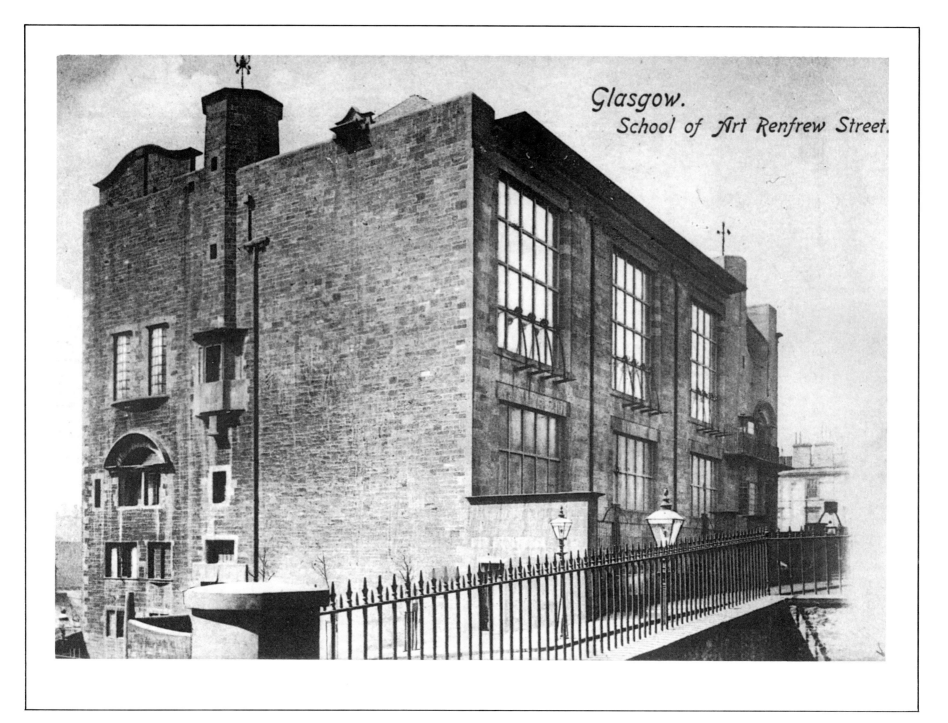

*85. Glasgow School of Art after the first phase of construction, 1897–99,
eastern and facade elevation. Photographer unknown.*

of the nineteenth century: "These days you can see crowds of people standing around this new building. They are office workers, workmen, women on their way to work, but instead they are stopped in amazement . . . they stare, they discuss this 'thing' they see being built . . . they think it strange, they have never seen anything of its kind, they don't like it, it repels them . . . and this goes on all day." This might easily have been written of Mackintosh's School of Art, but it is actually about the response to an equally "outrageous" creation built a year later than the School of Art, the Secession-haus by Josef Maria Olbrich in Vienna (1898). His structure, in a new non-historic language, suffered the same barbed commentary as his Scottish counterpart received from the uncomprehending. In Glasgow they asked what on earth was being built up there on the Garnethhill. What was that "strange edifice"? Was it a barracks; a factory; a new fortress; a poorhouse; a prison or place of correction; a temple of strange worship? It's all of these; it's an art school.

The opening ceremony of the completed eastern section of the building took place in December 1899. Mackintosh was not present and the contemporary newspaper accounts omit his name as architect, simply ascribing the work to the firm of Honeyman and Keppie. Financial constraints led to the building being erected in two stages, the first from late 1897 to 1899, the second (western) portion from 1907 to 1909. During the years between the harmonious joining of the two sections Mackintosh completed all his other major works in Glasgow. The School of Art was, in essence, the first and last of the Glasgow works of this astonishingly prolific man, spanning a period of heroic productivity. It is partly due to the time that elapsed between its beginnings in 1897 and its completion in 1909 that his interior work had matured, to culminate in a genuine masterpiece of interior architecture, the dark jewel that is the School's Library.

86. Glasgow School of Art, 1897–99, 1907–09, section and elevations, dated November 1910, pen and ink and watercolour.

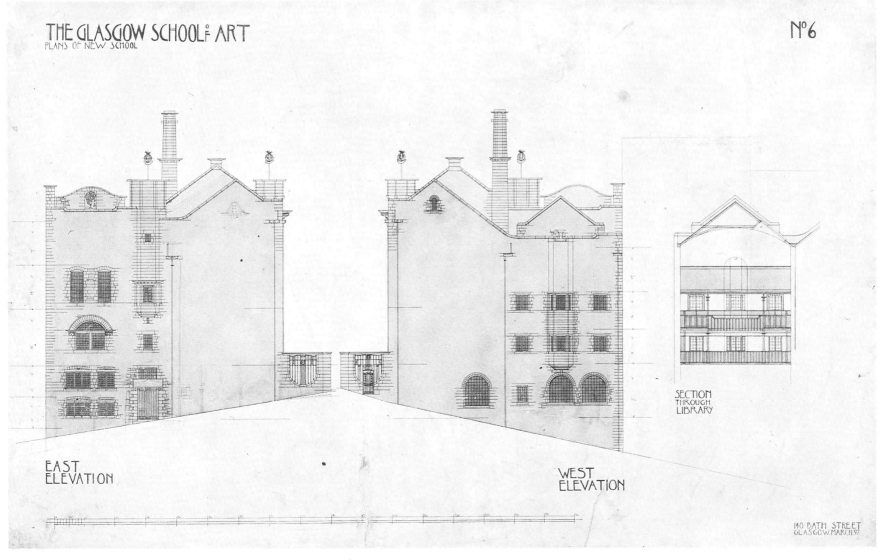

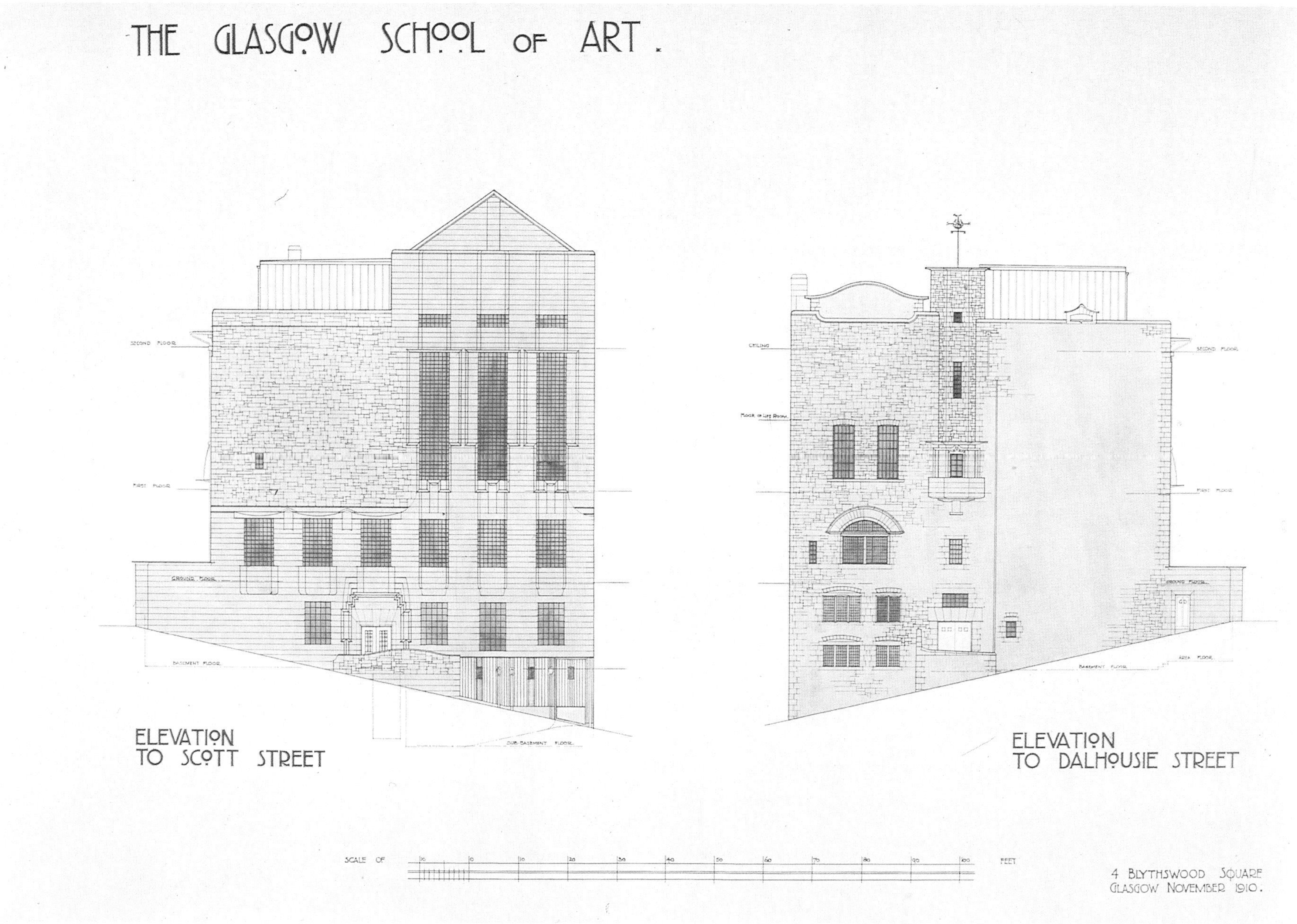

THE GLASGOW SCHOOL OF ART.

ELEVATION
TO SCOTT STREET

ELEVATION
TO DALHOUSIE STREET

4 BLYTHSWOOD SQUARE
GLASGOW NOVEMBER 1910.

87. Glasgow School of Art, elevations to Dalhousie St. (east) and Scott St. (west).

   The exterior of the building gives an early indication of the endless series of surprises and delights that Mackintosh conjured in his creation of the design. A particular example is the subtle asymmetry of the facade (many fail to notice it) and how delicately the contrast is balanced. Contrast is a clue to Mackintosh, and to his ability to manipulate one's experience of space, mass and flow, by creating a constantly changing series of counterpoints – high against low, rough against smooth, black against white, dressed stone against cement render, broad against narrow, gloom against blinding light. Throughout the School he uses such devices to entertain, charm and create environmental responses that are in accord with the purpose of the spaces. While Mackintosh revised the elevation drawings of the School several times, one of the most dramatic contrasts

88. Glasgow School of Art, western elevation, 1907–09.

89. *Glasgow School of Art, eastern elevation.*

90. *Glasgow School of Art, western elevation.*

91. Glasgow School of Art, the composition and plant drawing room.

Top of the western elevation, 1907–09 phase.

was included at the outset, the other during the hiatus between the eastern and western sections: the first, the marked contrast between the dressed stonework of the northern facade (and both of the side elevations), with the uncompromising severity of the southern

elevation; and the second, the contrast between the eastern elevation (1897–99), and the Library wing west elevation (1907–1909).

The eastern elevation clearly recalls castle

92. Glasgow School of Art, western entry doorway and enclosure wall.

93. *Maquette by Mackintosh for a bas-relief roundel over the entrance to the Glasgow School of Art, 1899.*

architecture, replaying devcices such as an attached tower, arrow-slit windows, a compendium of windows of differing sizes, depths and styles, all deriving from Mackintosh's sketchbook studies of vernacular architecture. The entrance door is protected by a low L-shaped wall which could be closed off to create a small compound for holding animals (a horse, cow, various dogs, a baby elephant, and a camel borrowed from nearby Hengler's Circus) before they were taken into the Animal Room that Mackintosh had specially created next to the

doorway for the "study of beasts". In this eastern elevation there is a sense of whimsy or playfulness in his confident juggling with the components of the well-defined square of the gable end. All of this is in contrast with the western elevation, which rises in a similar way but then soars like a fortress tower. Mackintosh here fuses his understanding of the totemic power of that Scottish form with his appreciation of the geometric and arithmetic logic of Japan, in the high narrow *shoji*-screen windows of the double-storey library within. At the top of the south-western elevation he cantilevers out a

94. Metal finial, eastern tower, wrought iron, 1897–99.

the almost subliminal articulation of shapes and spaces. The whole doorway is overscaled with an elaborate projected surround containing the deep-set, but quite modestly scaled, black doors. This hooded lintel is flanked at the top edges with "crow-steps" (partly in recollection of castle architecture, but perhaps also a memory of the frontispiece of Lethaby's book, which showed a great stepped truncated pyramid) and in its geometrication it anticipates Art Deco. The effect of the doorway is that of a massive figural presence with strongly mechanical overtones, attached to the small L-shaped arm of the courtyard wall. The portal here *is* the "guardian" (Lethaby again) and it extends that arm to gather you into the threshold of the building. Given that Mackintosh designed this doorway when his commissions were faltering and he was still the object of derision to many of his professional colleagues, perhaps the sense that he wanted to convey was that once you come within the ambit of that arm you are drawn into the building, a portcullis will descend, the doors will close and you will be in the company of friends in Mackintosh's haven, a protective environment secure from the Philistines outside.

Mackintosh's use of an anthropomorphic theme is also to be seen in the main entrance to the School in the centre of the north facade, where the steps leading up to the main floor are steeply pitched, very wide at the bottom but narrowing sharply, leading to the two tall and vertically stressed entrance doors. Looking from above, one clearly sees how these walls and steps can be read as welcoming and protecting arms as one enters the building. They can also be read as a drawbridge, as in castle architecture. The whole of the entrance staircase is bridged from the street level up to the main entrance level of the building, and there is a large gap under the staircase, so there are implications of a moat, as in a real castle.

The northern facade of the School is a synthesis of multiple influences and themes, all brought

small greenhouse in which plants were grown, a giddy perch adjacent to the Plant Drawing Room, with its Japanese *tori*-like complex of roof trusses. Nature was always at hand as an inspirational source.

To the calculated sobriety and rigour of the western elevation is added a particular detail of remarkable and unforgettable power, the doorway into the basement sculpture studios, an abstracted yet unusually anthropomorphic element in Mackintosh's work that demonstrates his ability to create a specific sense or reaction by

*95. Front fence of Glasgow School of Art, detail, showing one of the
metal roundels depicting stylized bird.*

under the controlling will of its creator. Certainly
there are hints of Mackintosh's familiarity with the
work of his contemporaries in England. Devices
used by Smith and Brewer in their 1895 Passmore
Edwards/Mary Ward Settlement building in
London, by C.F.A. Voysey in his published drawing
of "A Studio" and by Norman Shaw's New
Zealand Chambers, London, 1871, all make
paraphrased appearances cheek-by-jowl with the
arrow-slit windows of Scottish castles and the
heraldic *mon* of the Japanese clans. While this may
sound as if it would lead to a confusing jumble, this
is not the case. In Mackintosh's hands the
inexorable logic of his planning and the sureness
of his design skills yield a strongly structured
composition in which the elements are
harmoniously united but enlivened with delicate
counterpoint. The central entrance block with its
"drawbridge" steps leads up to the centrally hung
pair of white entrance doors with surrounding
black woodwork. Above the door is the sign for
the School with its street number (167 Renfrew
Street) in a typographical style devised by

Mackintosh, and above this the only piece of
architectural sculptural embellishment on the
whole building: two inward-facing female figures,
the muses of inspiration perhaps, each holding the
symbolic Glasgow rose that was the signature of
the Stylists. Above this is the balcony of the
Director's Room, and to its left the spiral staircase
tower with arrow-slit window ascends to the
Director's Studio, almost invisible from street level
behind a parapet wall, the whole vertical being
topped by a metal finial. The entire effect is very
much of a castle keep, with all the implications that
this building is a place of strength, a redoubt, a safe
haven, a santuary.

There is obvious evidence of the influence of
Japanese design in the exterior details of the
northern facade. The fence of black metal vertical
bars is set against a rolling curved wall (note the
reference to St Mary's Ward) and interspersed
along this fence are remarkable vertical forms: the
T-shape of a stylized tree, or flower, and rising
above it a single spar surmounted by a circular
device. These roundels in cut metal, each about
two feet wide, depict animal forms: a bird, a bee,
a caterpillar, a scarab beetle, a bat, etc. Mackintosh
took the traditional *mon* theme of Japanese family
heraldry and transmuted it to his own purpose.
Dr Kimura's analysis, indicating the commonality of
Mackintosh's abstraction of these insects and
animals with those of Japanese *mon* family crests,
is convincing. It is known that Mackintosh had
access to books of Japanese heraldry, and some
were in his own library. If there is a symbolic
meaning to the choice of this curious little
menagerie it is now lost to us.

Mackintosh had written that "the extraordinary
facility of our style is converting structural and
useful features into elements of beauty". The
northern facade contains a perfect example in the
elaborate metal brackets attached to the
stonework and arching up to lock into the mullions

96. Front fence with 'ladybird' roundel, and entrance doorway.

platform on which to place planks and ladders for cleaning the windows, but these long stalks serve also as a reminder of natural forms of inspiration set in gentle counterpint to the handiwork of humankind. From within the studios they appear as though invisible window-boxes had sprouted these fantastic steel flowers. Do they also have Celtic overtones, and a uniquely Scottish reference: are they Mackintosh's variation on the national weapon, the claymore sword with its elaborately wrought basket hand-guard? In a single instance we see the poetic and the practical ability of the architect to join together multiple layers of purpose within a single beautiful motif.

Plan and interior of the School of Art

"Le Corbusier once confessed that his desire in building was to create poetry. Mackintosh's attitude is very similar. Building in his hands becomes an abstract, both musical and mathematical."

Nikolaus Pevsner in *Pioneers of Modern Design.*

The plan of the building was of critical importance, for it would dictate the elevations. One contemporary observer was to note that the design indicated that all the "practical requirements have dominated the style of the building" (*Glasgow Herald*), meaning that Mackintosh was consistent in his quoted belief that he built from the defined purpose of the interior apartments outward to the walls. All activity in the building is fed off central large corridors which run east–west. The principal studios are to the north and service functions to the south; this is common to all floors. The technical studios were placed in the basement but given glazed pitched roofs to bring good light even into the depths of the building. In the final version of the plans, this basement housed the Decorative

97. *Glasgow School of Art, northern facade, metal brackets .*

of the painting studio windows. These brackets have been the source of endless speculation. They have an entirely practical purpose in acting as spring-braces for the huge windows, yet they seem to grow organically, like fantastic flowers – each one different – from horizontally thrusting branches with leaf-pattern flat plates attached. The plates and spars serve the function of creating a

THE GLASGOW SCHOOL OF ART.

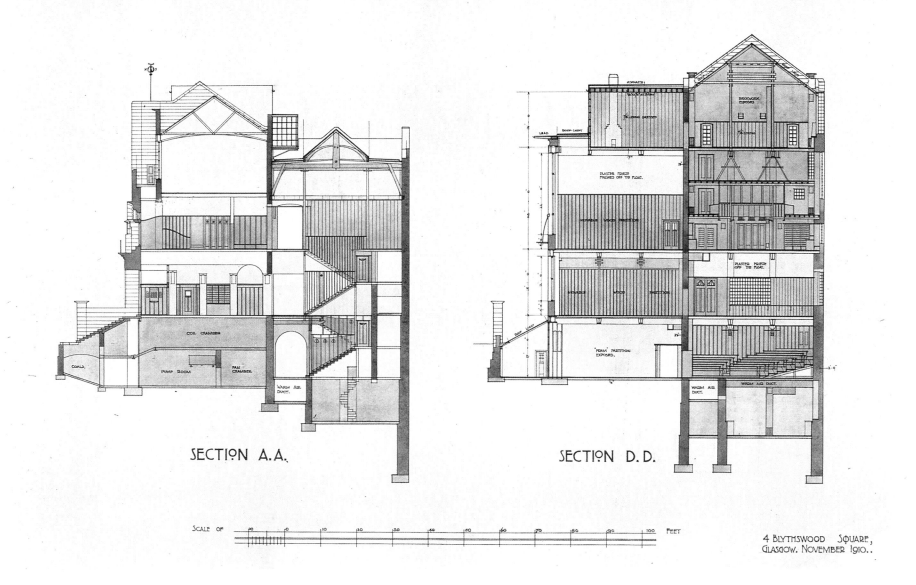

SECTION A.A.

SECTION D.D.

4 BLYTHSWOOD SQUARE,
GLASGOW. NOVEMBER 1910..

98. No 2 plan of Basement Floor, October 1st 1907.

The extensions are indicated by a wash

Arts Studios, which must have been close to Mackintosh's heart (silversmithing, ceramics, metalworking, stained glass, wood carving, enamelling, weaving and embroidery), and, from the first, his carefully designed Living Animal Room, a brilliant example of his determination to ensure that, in his own pursuit of perfection, he transmitted his beliefs to the students who occupied the building.

The Living Animal Room is the basement room in the north-eastern corner of the School, next to the exterior door protected by the animal pound enclosure. In order to preserve the flow of air through the building, Mackintosh designed what is in effect an airlock, in the form of a double set of double doors creating a barrier between the

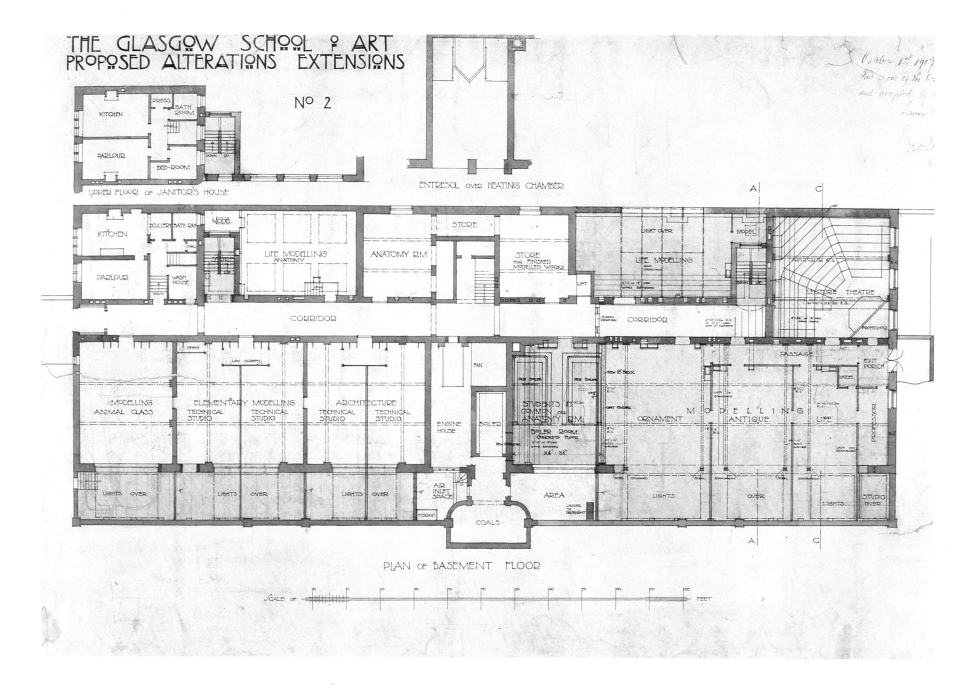

99. Section AA, Section DD, Glasgow School of Art Plans, 1910. Ink and watercolour.

outdoors proper and the actual corridor entrance into the School. Having come through the airlock, a larger animal such as a horse would be taken through very tall double doors, designed rather like Dutch barn doors, led into the animal class and tethered in the centre of the room. Students "sat on a raised platform that surrounded the animal, the animal droppings went into a floor drain, and pinned to the walls were charts of animal musculature and hanging from the ceiling, which

was very high, hung the skeletons of animals: we could firstly study those skeletons, then refer to the musculature charts and plaster models which were kept in the room, before then studying the finished living animal which we were modeling or drawing. We were told it was all designed especially for us students by Mr Mackintosh because he was so inventive. Mr Newbery even brought Mr George Bernard Shaw to see it." (Isobel Stewart.)

100, 101. The life modelling, casting and finishing studios, c.1910.

The basement also contained the mechanical mains that served the building and which also demonstrate Mackintosh's understanding and employment of new technology, such as forced-air central heating. The whole building is an exercise in the use of the materials and technology of the period: plate glass, steel trusses, timber produced through machine processes, and the use throughout of electricity for lighting and for allegedly the first master clock system (though Mackintosh had to wheedle the extra cost for "clean power" from the Governors). Mackintosh,

102. *Central staircase from the entrance lobby to the Museum, 1897–99.*

living witnesses, Mackintosh ingeniously designed a "well-tempered environment" for the occupants of the building: cold air was drawn into the building, heated and filtered, then pumped laterally and vertically through shafts in order to provide a warm environment with air from which the filth of the city had been removed. "We thought it an excellent building, so different from the others, very light and spacious, in a city so dirty and smelly from all the soft coal in the air, Mr Mackintosh's building was like Heaven to us." (Isobel Stewart.) The simple examples of the careful design of the Living Animal Room and the warm-air system may serve to illustrate a point vital in the consideration of Mackintosh: his determination to make the environment serve the needs of the building's occupants.

Though designed in 1896, the soundness of Mackintosh's planning and thought still serves the School's occupants well. It functions today as efficiently as it did when he created it. It is a building that presents itself to its occupants in a favourable way, and they respond to it because it is approachable, efficient, unambigious in presenting its purpose, well-planned and physically comfortable.

The main entry into the building is into a small vestibule, which acts as an airlock – a device common to all three entrances to the School. One enters a vaulted central lobby which, though spacious, has a generally low level of illumination, and progresses through the space as though being led forward to a staircase which is bathed in light from above. Mackintosh makes this staircase a veritable forest in the centre of the building.

The central staircase leads up from the entrance hall into the Museum, partly filled with plaster casts for drawing studies, with a pitched glazed roof flooding light into the interior. The scale recalls the Great Hall of medieval castles or baronial mansions, but the subtle detailing implies that the staircase is a living forest of vertical shoots (the wider balusters have a pair of leaf-shaped

who deeply respected Morris and Ruskin, certainly parted company with them in regard to the use of machinery, both as a technology in its own right, and as a means of making things. Ruskin had said in *The Lamp of Truth*: "All cast and machine work is bad . . . it is dishonest." Given the frightful pollution described in many contemporary accounts and by

perforations) culminating in four stylized "trees" that grow upwards to appear to support the canopy of the roof. The robust arched roof trusses with their Voysey-like heart-shaped perforations and Japanese pegging are in the stylized tree shape Mackintosh uses throughout the building. (The eastern elevation main window, the Director's Room window, the metal fence etc.,

all have variations of this same form as a recurrent motif.)

On the Museum floor (the first floor) the axial corridors lead to the great painting studios on the north wall. The ceiling height is about twenty-seven feet and a feeling of great spaciousness and flowing volumes is enhanced when the "accordion" doors (ten feet high) are pulled back to allow the

103. Glasgow School of Art, the Museum, first floor, 1897–99.

104. Glasgow School of Art, the Director's Office, first floor, 1897–99.

conversion of several principal studios into one huge room. (In these studios took place the balls, dinners and the lively and highly entertaining 'masques' for which the School became famous. Students, staff and the Newberys wore fancy dress to act out dramas and tableaux that they had written. Even the Mackintoshes attended these fund-raising events, on one occasion in the guise of Lancelot and Guinevere, roles that would obviously have appealed to their romantic literary sensibilities.)

The Director's Office is designed as a multi-purpose, open-plan space essentially square in plan, with a deep offset bay window to the west, the window itself again offset with the bay. The bay was intended to be the workplace of the Director (though the desk Mackintosh designed for him has only recently been created), served by a dumb waiter to deliver his mail, while the centre of the room, with its democratic round table, was used for more formal meetings. With Westdel (1898), this is one of the first of Charles' famous

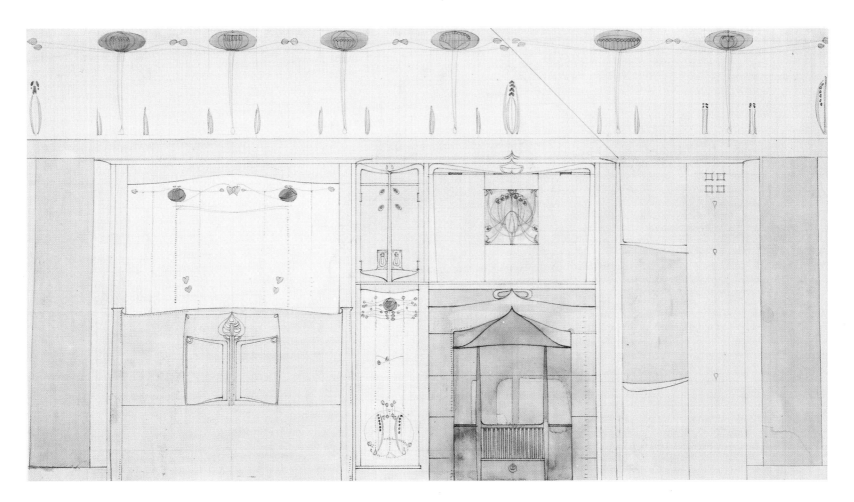

105. Design for a fireplace at 'Westdel', Glasgow, 1898.　　　　*Pencil and watercolour.*

"white rooms" that are imbued with a feeling of sensuous calm, accentuated here by the gently curving cornice at the top of the wall panelling which dips and flows into the bay window, and whose curves are replayed in the sweep of the panelling below the open screen of the spiral staircase leading up to the Director's Studio. Given that Newbery was a painter of note, and that spiral staircases pose difficulties in the moving of large canvasses, Mackintosh ingeniously created a long narrow trap door in the floor of the studio, with a block-and-tackle system to permit such works to be lowered down to the floor below. The Director's Studio contains a fine example of a fireplace – Mackintosh was a master of fireplace design – which, from contemporary accounts, seems was never needed: the warm-air system was so efficient that fires were redundant. The over-heating and dryness caused considerable comment: "We would rush to the tearooms as soon as class was finished and drink gallons of water . . . and we weren't allowed to open the windows either, it's what they called a 'sealed system' and janitors would come around to see we didn't do this because it upset the balance of the system." (Mary Newbery Sturrock.) This complaint is as common today of sealed system buildings as it was then. The room is notable for the way in which Mackintosh unites the design motifs of the grid pattern of nine squares, which became a *leit motif* for Mackintosh and which was also used widely by the Vienna designers under his influence. The grid is to be seen in the backs of the chairs designed for this room, and it is echoed in the legs of the circular table and again in the light fittings. It first appeared in his designs for the bedroom of Westdel. As with others of his projects the interiors were by no means furnished

106. *Design for the wall facing the fireplace at 'Westdel', Glasgow, 1898, pencil and watercolour.*

at the time of completion: "Fra" Newbery had to wait until 1904 for the furniture for the Director's Office, while the light fittings and Director's desk were installed by the author during the restoration of part of the School (1984–86), to the specification of the unexecuted drawings by Mackintosh.

The original Boardroom is a large open rectangle lit at either end by tall windows in shallow bays, the fireplace taking the centre portion of the southern wall. This high, wide, white panelled room unnerved the Board, who found it disturbingly clinical, and when the School's need for more studio space became urgent it appears they were happy to leave it for the more familiar

confines of the dark panelled Boardroom that Mackintosh created for them. The original Boardroom (now called The Mackintosh Room at the School) presently contains light fittings and some of the furniture from the Windyhill house, and a reproduction of the carpet designed for The Hill House. There is a special quality to the way light is handled in this long room. The windows face each other on the eastern and western walls, thus allowing light to flood into the room with a definite sunrise-to-sunset effect, but the symmetry was threatened when a new fireproof staircase had to be constructed, which threatened to blind the western windows. Mackintosh's ingenious solution was to place large windows in the outer wall of the staircase, then penetrate the central spinal wall of the staircase with arched openings, in order to bring light through these two barrier walls and still have it filter through the western windows, thus preserving the balance of the room.

The new Boardroom was created in advance of the 1907–1909 western addition and it perhaps pokes a little fun at the Board in its loose interpretation of Classical detailing, which would have surprised the staid architects of that body:

107. Glasgow School of Art, the original Board Room (now called the Mackintosh Room), 1897–99.

108. *The eastern windows of the Board Room, 1897–99.*

there had been constant friction between the Board and the architect, only the balm of Newbery's authority keeping hostilities in check.

The principal apartments of the School so far identified – the main studios, the staircase, the Museum, the Director's Office and the first Boardroom – stem from the original building of 1897–99.

Construction began on the western wing in

1907 and lasted until late 1909. Mackintosh's design for the northern facade wall retains continuity with the original elevation, though the western elevation is, as stated, in a far more rigid and geometricated style than he had conceived in the first draft of the plans. Mackintosh believed that architecture should be organic, and that his

109. *The staircase adjacent to the Board Room, east wing.*

plans were literally "anticipations" of "expectations", as the building would grow and change as it was built, by virtue of the interaction of those who erected it (a legacy of Arts and Crafts credos). The interiors of the 1907–1909

sections are, however, of an entirely different order and stylistically different from the eastern rooms. The focus falls on the magnificent sombre chamber of the Library, so often regarded as a masterpiece in its handling of scale, space, light and

110. *Glasgow School of Art, the second Board Room, 1906.*

atmosphere. The room is a place of great calmness and warmth, recalling the atmosphere of reverence and contemplation found in the great libraries of abbeys and cathedrals. The space is square, with the ceiling only partly supported by

slender vertical columns and beams, most of the weight being taken by vertical steel hanger straps attached to the steel crossbeams of the storage room above. The fascia of the gallery has wide panels that drop below its floor level as large

111. The Library, 1907–09, the central electric chandelier.

112. *Glasgow School of Art, the Library, 1907–09, the periodicals reading desk, 1910.*

pendants, each carved with a curious pattern recalling both an abacus and musical notation (the motif is used on the pilasters of the new Boardroom), which is repeated as a decorative element in the legs of the library tables, and on the large periodicals desk in the centre of the room. Each of these panels is different in its expression of permutations of the same theme. In both the general and the specific the interior shows

Mackintosh shedding himself of the sweeter sensual elegance of his domestic and Tea Room interiors, and concentrating on an interior of uncompromising severity and power. Radiating from the central chandelier (their design inevitably calls to mind miniature skyscrapers, while their geometric and architectonic qualities anticipate Art Deco by many years) pools of light alternate with shadows in dramatic theatricality. The overall

113. Glasgow School of Art, the Library, 1907–09.

effect is of a dialogue between light and dark, between horizontal and counterpoint verticals in an ambience uniting a Scottish sense with a Japanese tone.

R.D. Laing, the psychiatrist, theorist and educator, described his response after visiting the School and the Library: "The appearance of the Glasgow Art School . . . expresses the mind behind it. Here I feel that the tensions of the Scottish character find perfect synthesis: its wildness and austerity, its softness and ruggedness, come together in perfect proportion. It is a very congenial place to be in. Nothing in it cries out for attention, but everything is just right and it seems more right the more one looks at it. Correct without ever being cold. Those hanging lampshades are metal but they are not metallic. I wonder why the designers of our highrise

Somehow, he manages to take metal and use it organically and poetically to express through it light and colour and delight."

Queen's Cross Church

In 1898, during the construction of his School of Art, Mackintosh was entrusted with the design for a new church. It is perhaps a surprise that the tone of the building relates more to an interpretation of the Modern Gothic style, containing features in sharp contrast to the School's building (so utterly devoid of any such historicist references), though Mackintosh was to return to the adjusted Gothic style in his competition drawings for Liverpool Cathedral in 1903. The tower, however, recalls the interest he had in modestly scaled buildings and vernacular expressions in England – he has here adapted the tower of the Merriot Church in Somerset, which he had drawn in his sketchbook (21). Although a basically traditional approach to such a building, in which liturgical strictures define interior composition, it reflects Mackintosh's care for the spiritual and visual comfort of those using the church. The interior permitted him to experiment with a number of motifs later amplified in his designs for the western section of the School and the Haus Eines Kunstfreundes.

The 1901 Glasgow International Exhibition

Three years before the 1901 Glasgow International Exhibition, architects in the city competed to prepare designs for the construction of the buildings at Kelvingrove Park, for which the Honeyman and Keppie firm submitted designs by Mackintosh, though these were not chosen by the judges (James Miller's confection was the winning design). Mackintosh's designs were spare, elegant and rather festive – befitting their purpose – and

114. Glasgow School of Art, entrance from the lobby interior, 1897–99.

brutalism haven't taken a leaf from Mackintosh's book. But maybe they haven't loved, as he did, the flowers and plants that he spent so much time studying and drawing and painting as a boy.

in a style relating more to the School of Art building than to Queen's Cross Church. Of particular significance is the circular concert hall which predicts and anticipates by a number of years continental developments in the use of new technologies of steel, iron, glass and concrete. None of the designs was built and Mackintosh created only a number of small display stands and exhibition booths, and the White Cockade Tea Room for the International Exhibition.

115. St. Matthews Church, known as Queen's Cross Church, Glasgow, 1898, perspective elevation, pen and ink.

The Church is currently the headquarters of the Charles Rennie Mackintosh Society.

116. *Design for the Liverpool Cathedral Competition, 1903. Unexecuted.   Pen and ink.*

117. *Design for the 1901 International Exhibition, Glasgow, 1898.   Unexecuted. Pen and ink.*

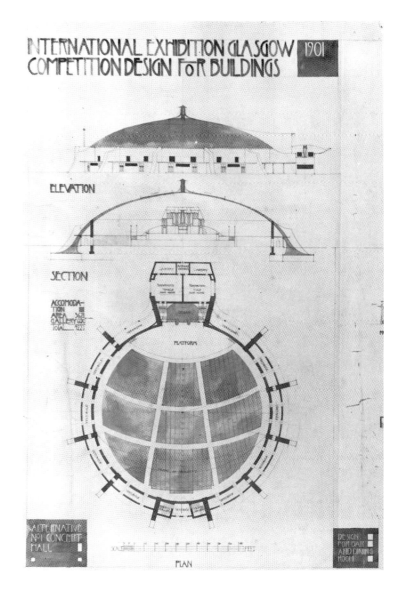

118. Unexecuted design for a Concert Hall 1901 Glasgow International Exhibition, Glasgow, 1898, pen and ink.

Mackintosh's domestic interiors

"There is no hope that our aesthetic cultural sense will prevail to allow such rooms to be accepted as normal. But they are milestones erected, in anticipation, by a genius, to demonstrate to Mankind the higher and sublime."

Hermann Muthesius, *Das Englische Haus*, 1904.

When Hermann Muthesius came from Germany to visit Mackintosh in the latter part of the nineteenth century, he certainly was not the first or the last major critic and commentator on contemporary art and design to have made the pilgrimage to Glasgow to see the work of Charles Rennie Mackintosh. From Vienna came Fritz Waerndorfer, later, Josef Hoffman, and later

119. Design for a Concert Hall for the 1901 International Exhibition, Glasgow, an architectural model of the unexecuted scheme.

121. Interior of the Mackintoshes flat at Mains Street, Glasgow, 1900.

Eduard Wimmer, all drawn to see Mackintosh by the substantial number of reports and illustrations of his work that were to be found on the pages of the leading British and central European art journals of the day.

Mackintosh and Margaret had married in 1900, and although they never actually designed and built a house for themselves, they converted a number of apartments and flats, and eventually a house, for their own purposes. The insertion of a Mackintosh

120. Detail of interior 120 Mains Street.

interior into an existing building was a complex act of retrofitting and conversion. The Mackintoshes lived in a style of simplicity and austerity that occasionally made Glasgow visitors wonder if their apartments were actually finished. They were indeed finished. The Mackintoshes "reduced" in both their style of life and their style of design. They reduced their needs to the simple and the absolute and also the remarkably beautiful. When Muthesius visited Mackintosh, he commented on the Mackintoshes' interior: "The severe and at the same time subtle atmosphere cannot tolerate the

122. *The dining Room at the Mains Street flat, 1900.*

intrusion of the ordinary. An unsuitably-bound book on the table would be a disturbance. People of today . . . are strangers in this fairy-tale world."

Most interiors in Glasgow at the turn of the century were cluttered with big plants, large ornate pieces of furniture, collections of art works and objets d'art, stuffed into oppressive overdressed interiors. The Mackintoshes rid their own interiors of all such excessive ornamental references, and their Glasgow interiors were the antithesis of the suffocating Victorian style. The words of William Morris apply perfectly: "Simplicity of life, even the barest, is not misery, but the very foundation of refinement." Given that in the 1890s Glasgow favoured the "obstacle course" style of Victorian interior decor, the chaste Mackintosh interior ensemble appeared austere in the extreme.

Contemporary photographs taken of the Mackintoshes' house at 178 Southpark Avenue

by the renowned photographer T.R. Annan reveal their continuing fascination for joining together Scottish and Japanese themes. In the photograph of 1903, showing the main fireplace of the drawing room at 178 Southpark, we see a large beaten lead fender with stylized plant forms, very much

123. The Drawing Room at the Mains Street flat, 1900.

124. *The Drawing Room at the Mains Street flat.*

in the Mackintosh manner, standing before a large and imposing fireplace, with its sweeping lintel and four small square recesses, two on each side, let into the surface of the fireplace. These contain, along with some books, some Japanese ceramic bowls, and there are two rice bowls on the lintel directly above the fireplace itself. On the shelf of the fireplace, the mantel, are dried flowers in the traditional Japanese style, and framed Japanese prints from Mackintosh's own collection.

The Mackintosh house was demolished, but it has been completely and beautifully reconstructed

125. *The studio fireplace, the Mackintoshes flat Bath St. Glasgow.*

126. *The Drawing Room fireplace, Bath Street flat.*

at the University of Glasgow (Hunterian Art Gallery) so that upon entering these apartments, completely furnished with the original furnishings, once again one can gain a sense of the quality of space and light that the Mackintoshes created for themselves. On the ground floor is an entrance hall, tall and narrow, and, as with all the apartments of the house, it has been carefully converted by Mackintosh from the original mid-Victorian terrace villa into a work entirely his own. Consistent with Mackintosh's interest in contrast, one is struck by the difference between the interiors in this house and its conservative genteel exterior. The hallway leads to the dining room, a space which, consistent with his interest in Japanese themes, concentrates all its decorative detail and display of artwork well below the picture rail. The space above the picture rail is painted white, the space below a deep sepia tan. The walls are covered on both the east and west sides with a stencil pattern tracery showing stylized roses against a garden trellis, with random dots of silver paint seeming to represent dew or raindrops falling from the roses. Mackintosh's drawing for this interior shows the chairs gathered around the table in a group of six. The chairs are high-backed with an oval top rail,

a stylized form of a flying bird penetrating the oval. (These chairs were also used in the Argyle Street Tea Rooms of 1895.) They create a room within a room, so that when dining with the Mackintoshes, one would be sitting in a separate enclosure as the core of the room itself. It was to this interior that Hoffman, Wimmer and Muthesius would have come to visit the Mackintoshes in Glasgow, not simply to partake in a meal with them, but to have been part of a communion of

128. Overleaf: The Mackintosh House: 78 South Park Terrace, the Drawing-room, cabinets, 1902.

127. The Mackintosh House
(Reconstruction of 78 Southpark Terrace)

129. *The Mackintosh House, studio Drawing-room, with table and chair.*

spirits who believed so deeply in the ideals of the modern movement.

The main salon of the house is on the first floor and comprises two rooms which Mackintosh joined together to create one open and somewhat L-shaped space. As the house was the end of a terrace, Mackintosh was also able to introduce new windows into the gable-end wall of the house. By using these windows with the existing windows, and by introducing pull-across curtains in an

oatmeal coloured cotton, he created an environment where he could not only modulate the nature of the light entrance space, but also, by means of these "temporary walls" in the form of curtains, alter the shape of the space.

The interior contains a number of the most striking pieces of furniture of Mackintosh's invention: most notably the two large white cabinets, designed by Charles and Margaret, flanking the main fireplace. The large lug-chair

130. The Mackintoshes house at 78 Southpark Terrace, Glasgow, in 1906. The photograph shows the studio/library, a writing-desk of 1904, a bookcase (left) of 1900, and an armchair of 1897.

131. *The Mackintosh Home, the Drawing-room. White chair of 1902, table (left) 1900, table (right) 1902), lug chair, 1900.*

is derived from Scottish themes, and it is of particular interest to note the way in which Mackintosh introduces stylized flower forms into the vertical upright supports on the face of the chair. Several of the chairs and tables, painted white, and with stencil patterning of stylized roses, were those seen in the Turin exhibition of 1902. Aside from the main space, there is a library area, which contained a collection of the Mackintoshes' books, and also in this space was Mackintosh's own

writing desk, and a black T-shaped *kimono*-like presence, which stands in negative/positive counterpoint to Margaret's writing desk, a white inverted U-shape with beaten silver door panels. The fireplaces are of particular interest: Mackintosh created one room with two fireplaces. The T-shaped form of Mackintosh's writing desk is repeated in the shape of the fireplace itself and, as with much of Mackintosh's work, there is a constant dialogue between forms, which is carried out on an almost subliminal level. To be noted with the fireplace are the two large grey cushions, one on either side of the fireplace, specifically designed for the Mackintoshes' two grey Persian cats.

The upper floor contains the Mackintoshes' bedroom. In the centre of the space is the cubic form of the four-poster bed, with awnings overprinted with stylized roses and other flowers. A central post in the footboard of the bed is penetrated with tiny elements of coloured glass, which, facing the east, cast shots of coloured light into the interior of the frame of the recessed bed area.

133. The Mackintosh House, the bedroom, cheval mirror, 1900.

134. The bedroom. Bed, 1900, silvered metal panel above fireplace by Margaret Macdonald Mackintosh, 1899.

Above the mantelpiece is a large beaten silver panel of stylized figures flanked on either side by flying cherubim. Of particular note is the powerful presence of two sets of large wardrobes, in which the stylized form of a bird is to be seen at the top of the doors, with the overstressed claws or talons of the hawk stretching down to the centre of the door and becoming the handles for the wardrobe doors. In the corner of the room is the remarkable

132. The Mackintosh House, drawing rooms and studio/library to left.

experienced both together: " . . . two visionary souls in ecstatic communion . . . wafted aloft to the heavenly regions of creation"; and, "On the second floor of a modest building in the great industrial smoky town of Glasgow there is a drawing-room amazingly white" (E.B. Kalas, 1905). Herman Muthesius' comprehensive summation was: "The whole world of interior decoration has been

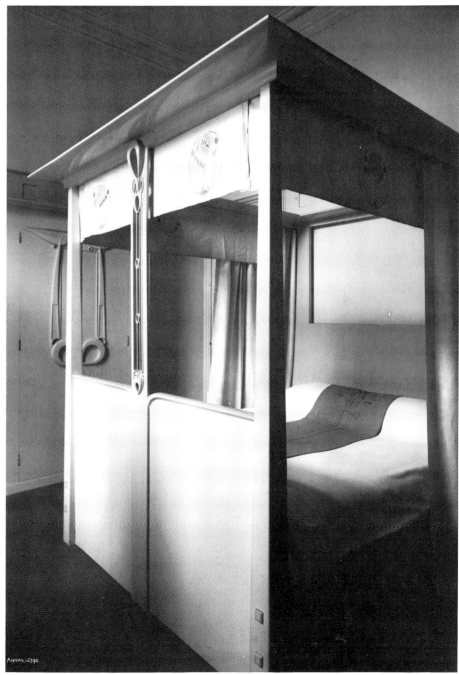

137. *The Mackintosh four-poster bed, 1900, for the Mains Street flat.*

136. *Detail of candle-holder wall scene from the dining-room, 120 Mains Street, 1900.*

and dramatic presence of the eight-foot high cheval mirror growing like an exotic bloom.

The impact of these interiors is difficult to convey, and the effect of the space, combined with the powerful personalities of Charles and Margaret, somewhat overwhelmed those who

135. *The Mains Street flat, 1900, the bedroom.*

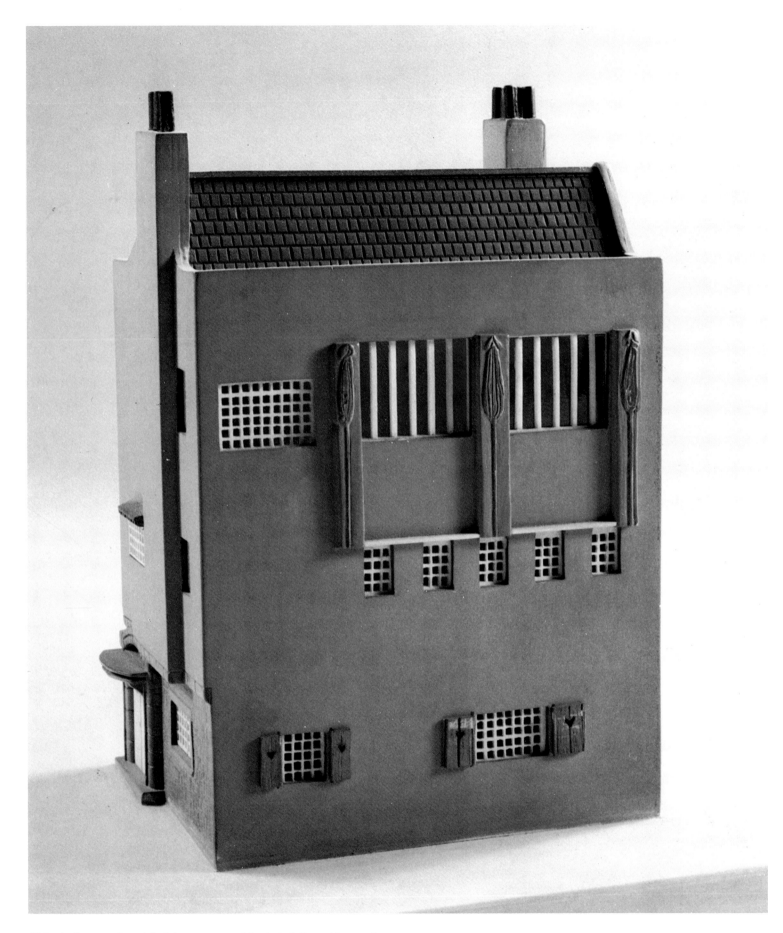

138. *Architectural model of the unexecuted An Artist's Town House of 1900–01.*

infinitely enriched by Mackintosh. Not only has he revealed new methods, he has upgraded their very concept."

Had Mackintosh's professional career been the success he sought and so deeply desired it is probably safe to speculate that he would have created new domestic premises for himself and Margaret. In 1901 he designed two strongly modelled houses "for an Artist". The first is A Town House, a three-sided three-floor

139. Design proposals for an Artist's Town House, 1900–01. Unexecuted.

140. An Artist's Town House.

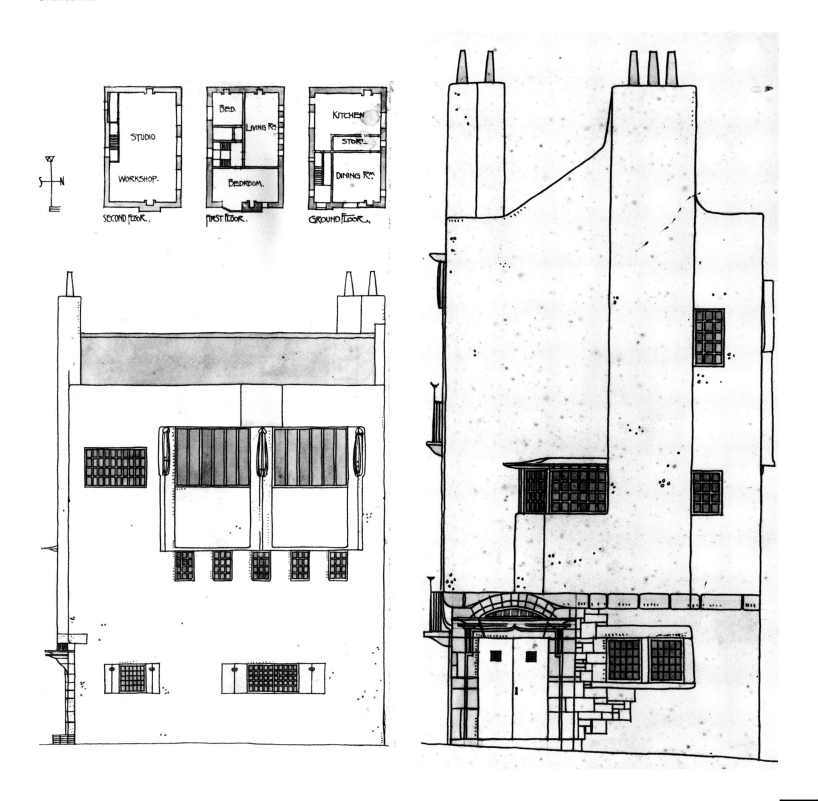

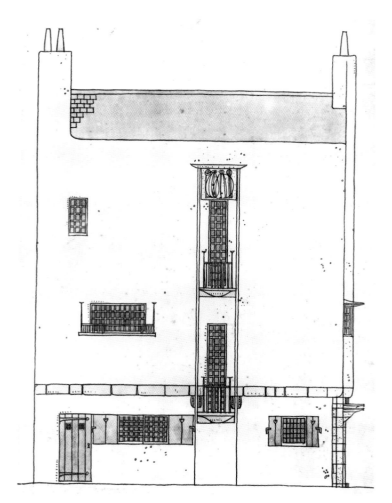

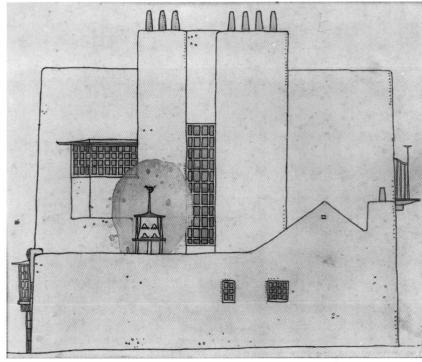

142. Designs for An Artist's Country Cottage and studio East Elevation 1900–01 (unexecuted) pen, pencil, grey and light green wash on cream paper.

141. An Artist's Town House.

143. Artist's Country Cottage and studio, south elevation and plan.

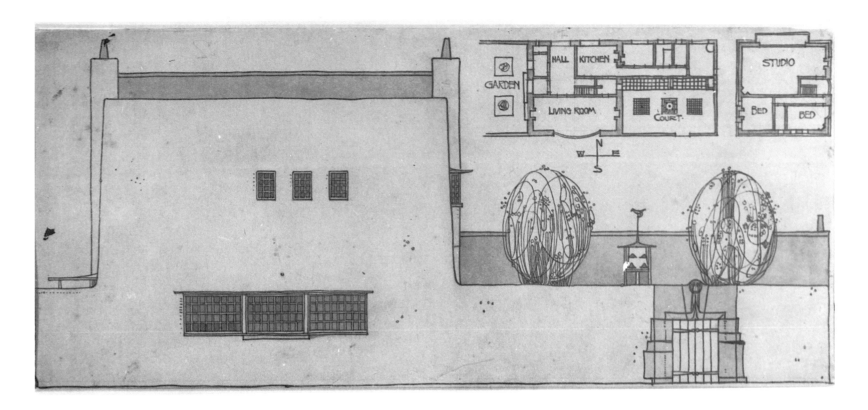

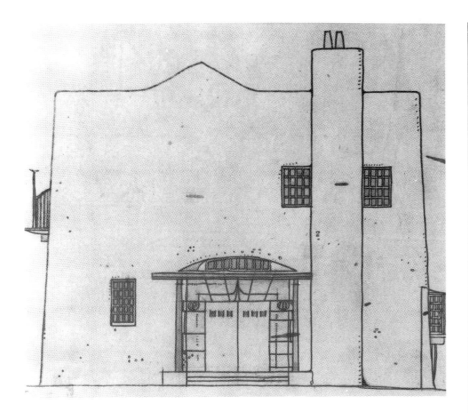

144. An Artist's Country Cottage and studio, west elevation.

vertically-stressed house intended for a city site, where its fourth side would abut an existing structure. The horizontally-stressed A Country Cottage incorporates a walled garden. Both designs show plans that include a studio, and there can be little doubt of the identity of the artist– dreamers who wished to reside in these properties.

Windyhill, 1899–1901; the *Daily Record* building, 1900–1901

During 1900–1901, Mackintosh designed the *Daily Record* building in a very narrow lane, a site that renders the building almost impossible to view. His elegant vertical watercolour perspective indicates the problems he was to encounter. The strong verticals recall the elongation of the motifs in the

145. The Daily Record Building, Glasgow, 1901, watercolour.

146. "Windyhill", Kilmacolm, 1901. Southwest perspective elevation.   *Pen and ink.*

147. "Windyhill", Kilmacolm, 1901. Northwest perspective elevation.   *Pen and ink.*

earlier graphic work, as well as in the School. The surface is neither stone nor rough-cast, but mostly of white ceramic tile rising to the attic storey, where sandstone is used for the dormers.
A strong rhythmic flow appears in the headings to the loading-dock doorways, again recalling the low facade wall at the School of Art.

As the first stage of the School of Art building was completed, Mackintosh received a commission from his friend William Davidson (for whom he had designed furniture for the Davidson home, Gladsmuir). This was the first opportunity for Mackintosh to create a free-standing domestic residence – Windyhill, Kilmacolm, near Glasgow. The drawings date from 1899–1900 and construction of the house took place in 1900–1901. Mackintosh rarely departed from the traditional construction techniques in common usage, and Windyhill was clearly consistent with Mackintosh's nationalist ethic, a Scots house for Scots people in a Scots climate. It retains, therefore, a character that derives from the simple

148. "Windyhill", Kilmacolm, 1901, the rear elevation.

149. Interior of "Windhill", Kilmacolm, 1901, the hall.

vernacular expression to be seen in traditional Scottish farmhouses, but here reduced and simplified. The austere robust massing was perhaps too Spartan for the Davidsons, for they attempted to relieve the sheer plainness of the southern elevation by adding shutters to flank the windows. Examination of the elevations of Windyhill in relation to the southern elevation of the School of Art indicates Mackintosh's preoccupation with the power of simple cubic volumes. There are large expanses of sheer vertical wall in counterpoint with small windows punched into the facade, apparently·at random, but directly related to the disposition of the interior apartments. The "harling" or rough-cast finish in pale grey emphasizes the starkness and

150. Interior of "Windyhill", Kilmacolm, 1901, the hall and staircase.

crisp angularity of the design, a finish that he had used with dramatic effect in the School of Art, and in 1902 when he designed The Hill House. The plans of Windyhill and The Hill House are very similar, an L-form derived, it is said, from his admiration of the disposition of plan in an 1893 Lethaby house, The Hurst, Sutton Coldfield, England. The Windyhill interior is Mackintosh's first true fusion of art and design within architecture of his own device, the whole recalling his belief that modern architecture was not simply to be an "envelope without contents". The work here stands as a prototype for the fuller expression to be seen in The Hill House. The light fittings and much of the furniture from Windyhill was placed in the collection of the Glasgow School of Art.

151, 152. *Light fittings at "Windyhill", 1901. Much of the original furniture and fittings from the house were gifted to the Glasgow School of Art and are in that Collection.*

The Hill House, 1902–04

"During the planning and building of The Hill House I necessarily saw much of Mackintosh and could not but recognize, with wonder, his inexhaustible fertility in design and astonishing powers of work. He was a man of practical competence, satisfactory to deal with in every way, and of a most likeable nature."

Walter Blackie, client for Mackintosh's The Hill House, 1904.

"Here is the house. It is not an Italian Villa, an English Mansion House, a Swiss Chalet, or a Scotch Castle. It is a Dwelling House."

Mackintosh to Blackie on "handing over" the completed Hill House.

Though his patrons were few, Mackintosh was fortunate to have formed a strong bond with those who commissioned him. The Glasgow publisher Walter Blackie was a thoughtful and intelligent client who wanted to create a new home for himself at Helensburgh, to the west of Glasgow, in 1902. His chief designer of publications was Talwin Morris, and it was he who introduced his employer to Mackintosh. Blackie was surprised at the youthfulness of the architect. Blackie visited Mackintosh's other works to review what had been provided for the clients, and the Davidsons' Windyhill house must have been a powerful influence. The apocrypha which surrounds Mackintosh tells of his "living with the Blackies' family to observe their way of life". Though this seems implausible, he did spend a considerable amount of time with his client reviewing the nature of the family's needs, as Blackie recalled: "He submitted his first designs for our new home, the *inside* only. Not until we had decided on these inside arrangements did he submit drawings of the elevations." Blackie had a decided view of what was wanted, but Mackintosh must have been somewhat surprised to find that his client's ideas were so absolutely akin to his

153. *"The Hill House", 1903, perspective elevation south- west.*   *Pen and ink.*

own. "I fancied a grey rough-cast for the exterior walls, and slate for the roof, and that any architectural effect should be secured by the massing of the parts rather than by adventitious ornamentation. To these sentiments Mackintosh at once agreed." The beautifully drawn perspectives indicate that the house varied little from the original plans through to its final execution.

The Hill House was to provide for Mackintosh some of the opportunities that would have been offered had the *Haus eines Kunstfreundes* been built, though on a more modest scale. That many of his contemporaries in Britain developed reputations founded on the creation of great

houses heightens the disappointment that Mackintosh created so few complete houses. The Hill House nevertheless ranks as one of the finest domestic creations of the period anywhere in Britain.

The exterior walls are "harled" in light grey and give the overwhelming impression of the vernacular tradition of Scotland, while the interior mingles Mackintosh's own sense of invention with a strong undertone of Japan in a brilliantly conceived interior–exterior contrast. The L-shaped plan creates a separation of purpose, with the main family living area to the west and a tower-like service structure (kitchens, children's room, storage, small servant's quarter, etc.) to the east and linked by the circular staircase tower, all robustly and directly Scottish in derivation. There is a playfulness in all this and a clever dialogue between the parts: in the garden is a miniature version of the staircase tower created for the gardener's implements.

All traces of the traditionalist themes of Scottish architecture, which Mackintosh so often paraphrased in exteriors, disappear in the interior of The Hill House. The ground floor entrance lobby and hall speak of his absorption of Oriental themes and their integration into his own idiosyncratic expressions. The drawing room was created as a large multi-purpose space which combined a brightly lit window bay and seat, a recess for a piano and a fine fireplace to create a friendly hearthside place within the room. The

154. "The Hill House", Helensburgh, 1903, southern elevation.

155. "The Hill House", Helensburgh, 1903, western elevation seen through the 'horseshoe' aperture in the garden wall.

ceiling, originally with a large kite-like lamp fitting, was eventually painted a deep damson/black above the picture rail (the finish colour was then "varnished" with buttermilk, which, when dried, gave a low-gloss sheen to the ceiling), which conspires to unify the whole ensemble and to give the distinct impression of a spacious lidless box, with all the studied theatrics of a dramatic stage set. Consistent with his love of nature, in the drawing room Mackintosh's window bay gives

156. Entrance Hall to "The Hill House", Helensburgh, 1903.

directly on to the garden and flows the house and garden together. Simultaneously, he brings nature into the house by means of a stencilled rose-and-trellis pattern (seen on the walls, in the stained-glass of the wall sconces and the shade of the standard lamp) used as a unifying design motif, while the recess to the left of the fireplace is a

tall stylized plant form which has grown into a bookcase.

Mackintosh's attention to the detail of the house was typical, for the moral imperative of his belief was that the architectural and design harmonics were the sole responsibility of the creator. The client, Blackie, wrote: "To the larder, kitchen, laundry, etc., he gave minute attention to fit them for practical needs, and always pleasingly designed. With him the practical purpose came first. The pleasing design followed of itself. Every detail, inside as well as outside, received his careful – I might say *loving* – attention."

The white bedroom is perhaps one of Mackintosh's most coolly elegant designs, the plan replicating that of the Director's Office of the School of Art, a square with an offset alcove (for the bed) with a vaulted ceiling. The woodwork, ceiling and walls are white, the latter with (originally) a light stencil variation of the same trellis seen in the drawing room below. The contrast of this richly pallid atmosphere with the hard black lines of the two ladderback chairs creates a fine dialogue of line and form, black calligraphy on a white sheet of space.

In his book *The Japanese House and its Surroundings*, Morse had described most British Victorian interiors in this way: "A labyrinth of varnished furniture with dusty carpets and suffocating wallpapers hot with some frantic design." The Mackintosh interior was the antithesis, a delicate and atmospheric richness conjured with the use of the minimum number of elements, the space animated by the calm sculptural presence of the furniture and by the living occupants, not by "some frantic design". The delicacy and care of the Mackintosh touch is to be seen in the southern exterior elevation of the white bedroom, where a convex wall bellies out from the flat plane of the exterior and Mackintosh places in its centre a small

157. Entrance Hall, clock, wall-stencils and chair, "The Hill House".
Helensburgh, 1903.

square window. Recalling castle architecture, he flanks this window with two protective shutters, but in The Hill House they are concrete recollections: they cannot move. Seeing them from the outside, however, one carries their memory inside to the white bedroom, where in that concave bay one finds the same small square window, now flanked with a pair of functioning curved shutters. Perhaps when the publisher Blackie rose each morning he opened those curved shutters, as one would open a book, at the dawn of a new day.

158. The Drawing Room at "The Hill House".

159. *The Drawing Room at "The Hill House", the window-bay.*

160. The Drawing Room at "The Hill House", showing a wall sconce,
stencil patterned wall, bookcase, and standard lamp.

161. *The White Bedroom at "The Hill House".*

162. *The White Bedroom at "The Hill House".*

163. The White Bedroom at "The Hill House".

164. *"The Hill House", exterior detail on the southern elevation.*

165. "The Hill House", exterior detail, southern elevation.   *The immovable "shutters" of the White Bedroom window.*

166. "The Hill House", interior detail, shutters of the White Bedroom.

The Willow Tea Rooms, 1903–1904

"Greens, golds, blues, white rooms with black furniture, black rooms with white furniture, where Whistler is worshipped and Degas tolerated."

Sir Edwin Lutyens

The 1903–1904 Willow Tea Rooms, Miss Cranston's showpiece, were designed from top to bottom by Mackintosh, though the building already existed as part of a bland terrace on busy Sauchiehall Street (Gaelic for "The Street of Willows"). Mackintosh "inserted" his four-storey, slim, white-painted Tea Room facade into the terrace and gave it a distinctive presence.

Mackintosh delineated the Willow Tea Rooms and separated it from its neighboring structures by the simple device of resurfacing the entire building, which he then painted white, and by running his characteristic checkerboard pattern up the edge of the building in order to separate it effectively from the flanking structures. Signboards indicating the name of the Tea Rooms again carried the familiar checkerboard patterning and his stylization

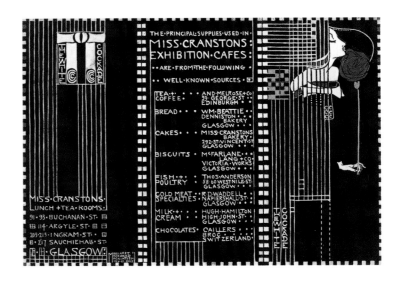

168. Menu card for The White Cockade Tea Room Restaurant.

of the coat of arms of the city of Glasgow: the bird, the bell, the fish and the tree. The interior was a triumph of the application of Mackintosh's idea of the "total work of art". With Margaret, he designed all the furnishings, including the curtains, wall panel decoration, tables, chairs, carpets, light-fittings and the menu, specified the cutlery and even attended to the dresses of the waitresses. Colour was restrained but rich, and the illumination by electricity, notably an incredible glass chandelier suspended like a dramatic electric

167. The Willow Tea Rooms, Glasgow, 1903–04, the facade (north).

169. Exterior signage for The Willow Tea Room, Glasgow, 1903–04.

171. *Interior of The Willow Tea Room.*

hanging basket of flowers in the centre of the main salon.

For the ground floor interior, Mackintosh designed one of the most famous of his pieces of furniture, the Willow Tea Room chair, (or settle), which was the chair of the manageress or cashier. The chair is a stylized but quite literal interpretation of a willow tree: the central vertical bars are the "trunk", the "branches" spread out and up to the top rail before they "fall" to the

170. *The front salon, The Willow Tea Rooms, Glasgow, 1903–04.*

half-round "pool of water" that is the seat. The chair is large, an imposing sculptural form which acted as a space-divider in the tea room, an imposing yet lyrical design.

The upper floor of the Willow Tea Rooms retains a Japanese sense of order and simplicity. Mackintosh removed a large portion of the roof and replaced the ceiling with stretched gauze or muslin which brings a gentle, flattering, shadowless illumination to the interior. As with much of Mackintosh's work, there is a marked contrast in the sense of space and light between the upper

172. *Interior of The Willow Tea Room.*

174. *The Gallery, first floor of The Willow Tea Room. Restoration of the interior undertaken by Keppie Henderson, Architects, Glasgow, in 1980.*

173. *Chair or 'settle', used by the cashier or manageress, 1904.*

175. *The Room de Luxe at The Willow Tea Room.*

and lower floors. The most luxurious part of the Willow Tea Rooms was the Room de Luxe, in which Mackintosh and Margaret created a partly mirrored-wall interior in silver, grey and pink. Entry is by means of a large pair of very elaborate stained-glass doors. The form is reminiscent of the familiar *kimono* shape which the Mackintoshes use in a number of their apartments, but here it is crowned with details based on natural forms, particularly the traditional Glasgow-style roses.

Mackintosh designed the flower vases, and legend has it that he often came to the Tea Rooms a few moments before it opened, so that he could arrange the flowers in the vases to ensure that the entire ambience was exactly as he desired.

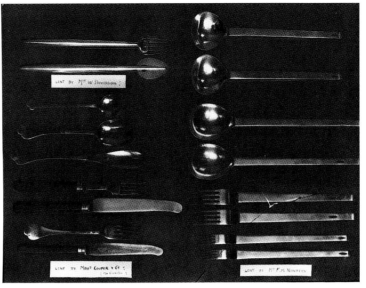

178. Silver plated cutlery for The Willow Tea Rooms.

176. Buchanan Street Tearooms.

177. Waitresses posed in The Room de Luxe.

179. Margaret Macdonald Mackintosh, gesso panel installed at The Willow Tea Rooms, 1903.

Scotland Street School, 1904–1906

On the completion of the building of The Hill House in 1904, Mackintosh continued to supply Blackie with interior furnishings and furniture for over a year, while simultaneously providing items for installation at the School of Art, the Tea Rooms, and for the domestic interiors. In 1904 he embarked on the redecoration of the interior of the home of Miss Cranston and her husband, Major Cochrane, Hous'hill, at Nitshill, Glasgow (destroyed by fire), a project that was to continue to 1909. The billiards room, the blue bedroom and the white bedroom are of special interest for the manner in which – as in his own home – he successfully integrated his characteristic total-design statement into pre-formed interiors without massive reconstruction or even an obvious attempt to obliterate references to the past. The Hous'hill commission was to provide an exceptionally rich and very large number of furniture pieces for the house in which the designer could explore new ideas, confident of the support and enthusiasm of a trusting client who was also a friend.

While the Hous'hill project continued, with characteristic energy Mackintosh pursued a number of other smaller commissions, although between 1904 and 1906 his principal concern was the erection of the Scotland Street School. That Mackintosh was astonishingly prolific has been alluded to several times, yet there is almost a sense of disbelief that he was capable of driving himself with such utter dedication to completing such a wide range of projects: The Hill House (1903–1904); a bedroom for the Dresdener Werkstaaten (1903); a continuing series of items to be installed at The Hill House throughout the years 1903–1906; furniture for the School of Art

180. Entry doors to The Room de Luxe at The Willow Tea Rooms.

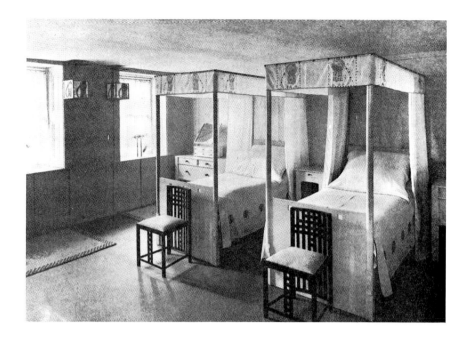

181. "Hous'hill", Nitshill, Glasgow, 1904, the home of Miss Kate Cranston, the White Bedroom.

182. "Hous'hill", Nitshill, Glasgow, 1904, the Music Room.

over the same period; Hous'hill (1903–1904), with later additional furniture up to 1909; furnishings for the Holy Trinity Church, Bridge of Allan (1904); a dining room for exhibition by A.S. Ball in Berlin (1905); the western extension of the School of Art (1907–1909); purchasing and remodelling the entire interior of the Mackintoshes' home at 78 Southpark Avenue (1906); the Dutch Kitchen at the Argyle Street Tea Rooms (1906); the Auchenibert and Mosside houses (1906).

Scotland Street School was designed in 1903 and built during 1904–1906 in a soft red sandstone. The northern (facade) elevation shows Mackintosh continuing to develop his own vocabulary with "quotations" from his favoured historic sources demonstrated in entirely new ways, the most dramatic being the use of two large circular-plan staircase towers, each with a conical roof, recalling castle forms, but with the solid walls and arrow-slit windows absent. They are replaced by a curved glazed screen that runs up the height of four floors to flood light into the main circulation areas. The two towers are for segregation by sex, boys to the right, girls to the left, a practice he was familiar with from his design of Martyr's Public School. Between the towers on the ground floor centre of the facade is a small-scale entrance for infants, humanely designed, it is said, especially for the wee ones

183. The Argyle Street Tea Rooms, Glasgow, 1906, the Dutch Kitchen.

184. *Scotland Street School, Glasgow, 1905–06, perspective elevation.*   *Pen and ink, 1904.*

who might be intimidated by the scale and rambunctious jostle of the large towers and the older children. The ground-floor gymnasium-cum-assembly hall is decidely Spartan and bears an interesting resemblance to the antiseptic interiors of Josef Hoffmann's Purkersdorf Sanitarium, while the staircase towers are persistently considered to have been influential on a number of architects of "the machine age", especially Walter Gropius, whose Cologne exhibition hall of 1914 bears more than a superficial relationship to Scotland Street School. In many ways Scotland Street School may be considered a hinge between the dynamics of the School of Art, the sensuousness of the Tea

Rooms and all the domestic interiors, and it presages the geometric abstraction of the School of Art's western doorway and the Derngate interiors of 1916. The elaborate thresholds and elongated windows recall the sculptural massing of the School of Art's western elevation, and there is a simple yet telling contrast between the bas-relief over the Art School's doors (1897) and the stylized flower forms on the Scotland Street southern entrance of 1904.

185. Scotland Street School, Glasgow, 1905–06, the southern facade.

186. Scotland Street School, Glasgow, 1905–06, detail of the
southern elevation.

78 Derngate, Northampton, England, 1916

Number 78 Derngate was commissioned by W.J. Basset-Lowke in 1916, by which time the Mackintoshes had moved to London. The house was contained in an undistinguished Victorian terrace, but, as with his insertion of "The Willow" into a bland block in Glasgow, Mackintosh reshaped the facade and, in quite astonishing contrast, enthusiastically remodelled the back elevation (a recollection of the School of Art) in a manner that could have been easily integrated into the works of his Viennese colleagues, or even the later Bauhaus, without a jarring note being struck. The house is very small, a stack of rooms on a sloping site, and what Mackintosh created in these

187. The hall, 78 Derngate, Northampton, 1916.

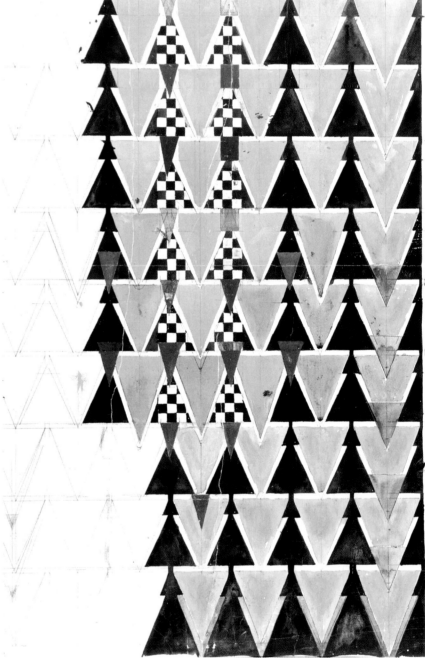

188. Derngate stencil design for wall.

tiny apartments was undertaken with an ingenuity that is exceptionally impressive. The ground floor layout was substantially altered by the relocation of the staircases, but the plan was necessarily constrained, and Mackintosh's sense of invention is all the more impressive because of these constraints.

Although the overall effect of an interior in which almost every surface – including the ceiling – was black could be anticipated as being overwhelmingly gloomy, this was apparently not the case, and a sense of "mystery and spaciousness" was the keynote. Eventually, however, the Bassett-Lowkes decided to lighten the interior and Mackintosh undertook to do so with a pleasing but much less distinctive result. The furniture was simple and bold, all in black with inserts of brightly coloured shapes in early plastics.

189. The hall, 78 Derngate.

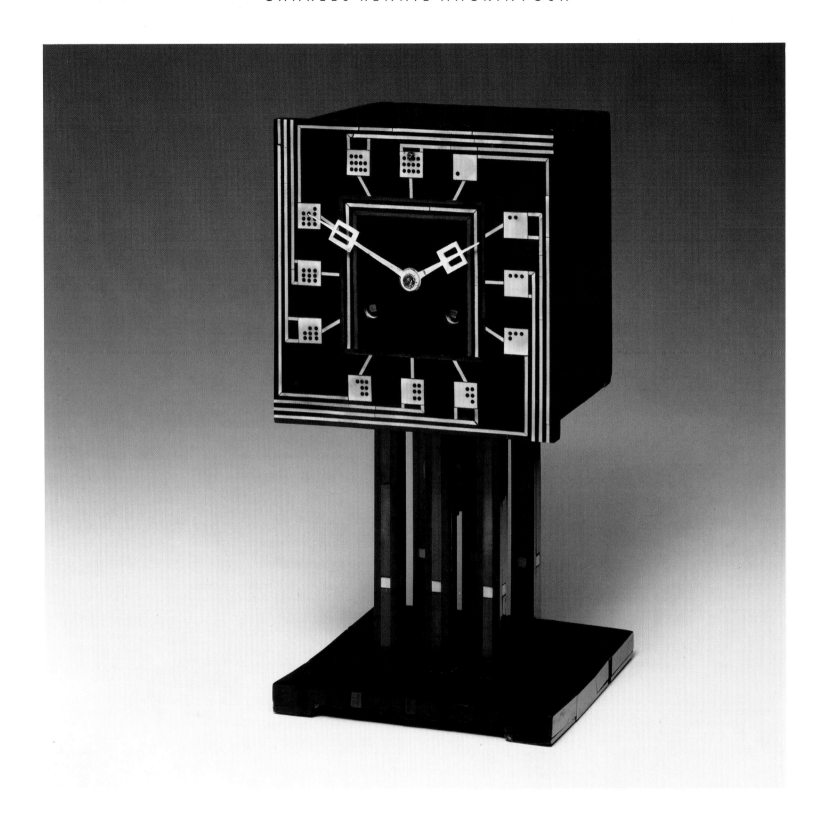

190. Clock for 78 Derngate, 1917, known as the 'domino clock'.   *Ebonised wood with Erinoid plastic inlay.*

Some of the furniture was made (exceptionally well) by German or Italian prisoners of war interned at camps on the Isle of Man.

The contrasts between the Glasgow white-on-white interiors and the black-on-black scheme

of Derngate could not be greater. The sensuous flowing line of Glasgow has been transmuted

191. The bedroom, 78 Derngate, Northampton, 1916, reconstructed at the Hunterian Art Gallery, University of Glasgow.

to a rigid geometrication that is sharp, hard and pointed, with wallpaper – not stencils – that contains grid patterns in interlocking triangles in red, white, green and yellow, colours that are restated in details of the otherwise entirely black furniture. The stylized flowers of the Glasgow

period are totally absent.

The combination of forms and colours anticipate the linear grammar of Art Deco and the International Style that was to develop in succeeding decades, and relates to themes Mackintosh had begun to explore in the Cloister Room and the Chinese Tea Rooms of 1911 at Miss Cranston's Ingram Street Tea Rooms. The guest bedroom shows Mackintosh utilizing the flowing lines of the early Glasgow period replayed in a taut and striking new manner, the alternating blue/black/white stripes running up the vertical contours of the furniture, through the counterpanes of the beds, up the headboard wall, on to the ceiling and then returning down the walls, while the grain of the mahogany shows

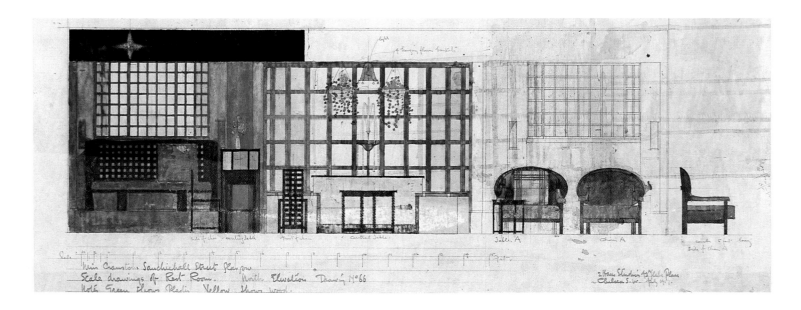

192. *Designs for The Dug-out at The Willow Tea Rooms, 1917, watercolour.*

193. The Chinese Room at The Ingram Street Tea Rooms, Glasgow, 1911.

through a clear finish and insert colours created by the use of plastics. In the tiny Derngate interiors, Mackintosh seems to repay a debt to his friends in Vienna. Certainly the garden elevation could be mistaken for Adolf Loos or Josef Hoffmann, and the interior detailing recalls Josef Urban, but the real homage here is the addition in 1919 of a large pendulum-driven mantle-clock which is unquestionably based on a clock by the Werkstatte designer Otto Prutscher. Mackintosh

provided in this interior exactly what the client had in mind; Bassett-Lowke described it as "distinctly futurist in character". It was eventually published in *Ideal Home* in 1920 but, as when the School of Art had opened, the name of the architect was omitted from the article.

194. Overleaf: Charles Rennie Mackintosh, photograph c.1920.

CHRONOLOGY

1864 Margaret Macdonald born.

1868 Charles Rennie Mackintosh born.
Herbert Macnair born.

1873 Frances Macdonald born.

1884 Mackintosh enters the architectural practice of John Hutchison as an apprentice. Enrolls as a part-time student at the Glasgow School of Art.

1885 –88 Awarded prizes at the School, two prizes by the Glasgow Institute of Architects, a bronze medal at South Kensington, London, two prizes by the Glasgow Institute.

1889 Joined the architectural practice of Honeyman and Keppie, continuing as a student at the School of Art. Wins a Queen's Prize at South Kensington, Design Prize at Glasgow Institute.

1890 Designs cabinet for his own use and 'cats' frieze at the family home. Wins the Alexander 'Greek' Thomson Travelling Scholarship with a design for 'A Public Hall'. Designs 'Redclyffe House'. Silver Medal at South Kensington, for the design for a museum of art and science.

The Macdonald sisters enter the Glasgow School of Art 1890–91.

1891 Tour of Italy, via London and Paris. Delivers a lecture on 'Scotch Baronial Architecture' to the Glasgow Architectural Association.

1892 A lecture on 'Italy' for the Glasgow Architectural Association. Enters the Soane Medallion Competition with designs for 'A Chapter House' which earns a Gold medal.

1893 Honeyman and Keppie design for the Glasgow Herald building, Mackintosh an active participant in the design. Drawings for 'A Railway Terminus'. A lecture on 'Architecture' for the Glasgow Institute of Architects.

1894 Hall and library at Craigie Hall. Drawings for Queen Margaret's Medical College.

1895 Drawings for Martyr's Public School. Interior works at 'Gladsmuir', Kilmacolm, for the Davidsons. Lennox Castle Inn, Lennoxtown.

1896 Poster for 'The Scottish Musical Review'. The competition for the new Glasgow School of Art announced, won by Mackintosh. Interior work at Buchanan Street Tea Rooms with George Walton, commissioned by Miss Cranston. Exhibits in London.

1897 Construction on the first phase of the School of Art (1897–99). Queen's Cross Church designed and built (1897–99). Furniture for the Argyle Street Tea Rooms. Work featured in 'The Studio' magazine. The Music Room organ case at Craigie Hall.

1898 Drawings for the 1901 Glasgow Exhibition. Work published in *Dekorative Kunst* magazine. Ruchill Street Church Hall. Dining-room commissioned by Bruckmann in Munich, Germany. White bedroom at 'Westdel' house, Glasgow.

1899 Frances Macdonald married Herbert MacNair. Designs for 'Windyhill' house, Kilmacolm, commissioned by William Davidson.

1900 Margaret Macdonald marries Charles Rennie Mackintosh. Interiors and furniture for Dunglass Castle, Bowling, for the Macdonald family. Interiors at the Ingram Street Tea Rooms (The White Dining Room) and at the Mackintoshes home at 120 Mains Street, Glasgow. Waerndorfer visits Mackintosh in Glasgow, invitation to exhibit at the Eighth Secession Exhibition in Vienna. The Mackintoshes visit Vienna, meet Hoffman, Olbrich.

1901 Additions to the Ingram Street Tea Rooms. 'Windyhill' house completed. Drawings for unexecuted 'A Town House for an Artist' and 'A Country Cottage for an Artist'. 'Daily Record' building. Designed exhibition stands at the International Exhibition. The Gate Lodge. Submits works to the *Haus Eines Kunstfreundes* competition. Kingsborough Gardens, Glasgow, interior commissioned by Mrs. Rowat.

1902 Exhibits at the International Exhibition of Modern Decorative Art, Turin, Italy. Travels to Italy with 'Fra' Newbery, Director of the Glasgow School of Art, Drawings for the Liverpool Cathedral competition. Commissioned by Waerndorfer to create a Music Room in Vienna. *Haus Eines Kunstfreundes* portfolio published by Koch, Darmstadt, Germany. Illustrated articles on Mackintosh in German publications.

1903 Drawings for 'The Hill House', Helensburgh, commissioned by Walter Blackie. Exhibits in Moscow. Design of The Willow Tea Rooms.

1904 'The Hill House' under construction. Interiors for 'Hous'hill' commissioned by Miss Cranston. Interior furnishings for Holy Trinity Church, Bridge of Allan 'The Willow Tea Rooms' opens. Upon the retirement of Honeyman, Mackintosh is made a partner in the firm. Designs for Scotland Street School (built 1904–06). Eliel Saarinen visits Glasgow.

1905 Articles on 'The Hill House' and 'The Willow' in German magazines. Dining-room for A.S. Ball in Berlin, Germany. Continuous design of furnishings for 'The Hill House', the Tea Rooms, 'Windyhill' and 'Hous'hill'.

1906 New Board Room for the School of Art. The
–07 Mackintoshes move to 78 Southpark Avenue. Drawings for the west wing of the School of Art. 'Mosside', Kilmacolm and 'Auchenlbert', Killearn, houses. 'The Dutch Kitchen' at Argyle Street Tea Rooms, 'The Oak Room' at the Ingram Street Tea Rooms.

1907 Construction of the west wing of the School of Art (1907–09). Extensions to 'The Moss', Dumgoyne, Killearn. Doorway to the Lady Artists Club, Glasgow. Visits Portugal.

1908 Further interior work at 'Hous'hill', extensions
–10 to Mosside house, 'The Oval Room' and interiors at the Ingram Street Tea Rooms.

1911 'The Cloister Room' and 'The Chinese Room' at Ingram Street Tea Rooms. 'The White Cockade' restaurant at the Glasgow Exhibition.

1913 Alterations to 'Mosside' house. Leaves Honeyman, Keppie and Mackintosh practice.

1914 The Mackintoshes leave Glasgow, move to Walberswick, England. Flower and landscape studies.

1915 Move to Chelsea, London. Fabric designs for
–16 Foxton and Sefton.

1916 78 Derngate, Northampton, interiors and exterior remodelling, commissioned by W.J. Bassett-Lowke.

1917 Bedroom for S. Horstman, Bath, and furniture for F. Jones, Northampton. 'The Dug-Out' at 'The Willow Tea Rooms', Glasgow.

1918 A cottage for the photographer E.O. Hoppe at East
–19 Grinstead. Mackintosh sells the Glasgow house at 78 Southpark Avenue to William Davidson. Interior designs and furnishings for Candida Cottage, Roade, for W.J. Bassett-Lowke, also the striped bedroom at 78 Derngate.

1920 Continued furniture and interior works for Bassett-
–25 Lowke. Unexecuted designs for studios in Chelsea for Arts League of Service, and a theatre design for Margaret Morris. Book covers commissioned by Blackie in Glasgow. Move to Port Vendres, France, 1923, where Mackintosh works on watercolour painting.

1927 Return to London. Mackintosh diagnosed as suffering cancer of the tongue.

1928 Charles Rennie Mackintosh died.

1933 Margaret Macdonald Mackintosh died.

LIST OF THE ILLUSTRATIONS WITH CREDITS

The publishers would like to thank the following for their kind co-operation in the research of material for this book and their permission to use photographs from their collections:

Mr Douglas Annan, T & R Annan & Sons, 164 Woodlands Road, Glasgow, Scotland.

Ms Pamela Robertson, The Hunterian Art Gallery, The Mackintosh Collection, University of Glasgow, Gilmorehill, Glasgow, Scotland.

Mr Peter Trowles, The Mackintosh Collection, Glasgow School of Art, 167 Renfrew Street, Glasgow, Scotland.

Mr Brian Blench, Department of Decorative Art, Art Gallery and Museum (Glasgow Museums and Art Galleries), Kelvingrove, Glasgow, Scotland.

Thanks also to Ralph Burnett, photogapher, and to **Elizabeth Carmichael,** Librarian of the Mitchell Library in Glasgow.

For the purposes of this list, **T&R Annan & Sons** is abbreviated to Annan, **The Hunterian Art Gallery** to **H.A.G.** and **The Mackintosh Collection, Glasgow School of Art** to G.S.A.

---

60. (p. 67) Theatre designs for Margaret Morris. *H.A.G. 44.0 × 72.0 cm.*

61. (p. 67) Theatre designs for Margaret Morris. *H.A.G. 44.6 × 72.1 cm.*

62. (p. 68) The Castle, Holy Island. *H.A.G. 26 × 20 cm.*

63. (p. 69) Stained glass panel. *H.A.G.*

64. (p. 71) Le Fort Maillert. *G.S.A. Photograph by Roger Billcliffe. 35.8 × 28.5 cm.*

65. (p. 72) Wall clock for the Glasgow School of Art. *G.S.A.*

66. (p. 72) An aphorism by J.D. Sedding. *H.A.G.*

67. (p. 73) The signboard over the G.S.A. entrance doors. *Photograph by Ralph Burnett.*

68–75. (pp. 75–82) Photographs of the Memorial Exhibition. *Annan.*

76. (p84) The Glasgow Herald Building. *H.A.G.*

77. (p85) Bookplate for John Keppie. *G.S.A.*

78. (p. 86) Queen Margaret Medical College. *H.A.G. 50 × 80.6 cm.*

79. (p. 87) Martyr's Public School. *H.A.G. 61.3 × 92.5 cm.*

80. (p. 89) Glasgow School of Art, northern and western elevations. *Photograph by Ralph Burnett*

01. (p. 90) Glasgow School of Art, watercolour. *G.S.A. 57.5 × 91 cm.*

82. (p. 91) Glasgow School of Art, South elevation. *G.S.A. 60.5 × 86 cm*

83. (p. 92) Glasgow School of Art, architectural model. *G.S.A. Photograph by Ralph Burnett.*

84. (p. 93) Glasgow School of Art, architectural model. *G.S.A. Photograph by Ralph Burnett.*

85. (p. 94) Glasgow School of Art, first phase of construction. *G.S.A.*

86. (p. 95) Glasgow School of Art, watercolour. *G.S.A. 60.5 × 80.5 cm.*

87. (p. 96) Glasgow School of Art, eastern elevation. *G.S.A.*
   (p. 96) Glasgow School of Art, western elevation. *G.S.A.*

88. (p. 97) Glasgow School of Art. *Annan.*

89. (p. 98) Glasgow School of Art. *G.S.A.*

90. (p. 99) Glasgow School of Art. *G.S.A.*

91. (p. 100) Plant drawing room, *G.S.A.*

92. (p. 101) School's western entry doorway. *Annan.*

93. (p. 102) Maquette over the doorway. *Photograph by Ralph Burnett.*

94. (p. 103) Metal finial, *G.S.A.*

95. (p. 104) Front fence of the School, detail. *Photograph by Ralph Burnett*

96. (p. 105) Front fence of the School. *Photograph by Ralph Burnett.*

97. (p. 106) Metal brackets on studio windows. *G.S.A.*

98. (p. 107) Glasgow School of Art plans. *G.S.A. 58 × 86.3 cm.*

99. (p. 108) Glasgow School of Art plans. *G.S.A. 60.5 × 80.5 cm.*

100. (p. 109) The life-modelling studio, *G.S.A.*

101. (p. 109) The life-modelling studios. *G.S.A.*

102. (p. 110) The central staircase, *G.S.A. Photograph by Ralph Burnett.*

103. (p. 111) The museum, *G.S.A.*

104. (p. 112) The director's office, *G.S.A. Photograph by Ralph Burnett*

105. (p. 113) Design for fireplace at Westdel. *H.A.G. 23.6 × 42.8 cm.*

106. (p. 114) Design for wall at Westdel. *H.A.G. 23.5 × 43 cm.*

107. (p. 115) The Mackintosh Room, *G.S.A. Photograph by Ralph Burnett*

108. (p. 116) The Board Room, *G.S.A. Photograph by Ralph Burnett.*

109. (p. 117) Staircase, *G.S.A. Annan.*

110. (p. 118) The Board Room, *G.S.A.*

111. (p. 119) The library chandelier, *G.S.A.*

112. (p. 120) The Library. *G.S.A.*

113. (p. 121) The Library. *G.S.A.*

114. (p. 122) The entrance doors, *G.S.A. Photograph by Ralph Burnett*

115. (p. 123) St. Matthews Church (Queens Cross Church). *H.A.G. 56 × 61 cm.*

116. (p. 124) Design for the Liverpool Cathedral. *H.A.G. 62.8 × 91.5 cm.*

117. (p. 124) Design for the 1901 International Exhibition. *G.S.A. 90 × 103 cm.*

118. (p. 125) Design for the Concert Hall. *H.A.G. 90.3 × 153.2 cm.*

119. (p. 125) Design for the Concert Hall, architectural model. *G.S.A. Photograph by Ralph Burnett.*

120. (p. 126) Detail of interior, Mains Street. *Annan.*

121. (p. 127) Interior, Mains Street. *Annan.*

122. (p. 128) The dining-room, Mains Street. *Annan.*

123. (p. 129) The Drawing-room, Mains Street. *Annan.*

124. (p. 130) The Drawing-room, Mains Street. *Annan.*

125. (p. 131) The fireplace in the studio, Bath Street. *Annan.*

126. (p. 132) The fireplace in the drawing-room, Bath Street. *Annan.*

127. (p. 133) The dining-room, Southpark Terrace. *H.A.G.*

128. (p. 134) The drawing-room cabinets, Southpark Terrace. *H.A.G.*

129. (p. 135) The studio/drawing-room, Southpark Terrace. *H.A.G.*

130. (p. 136) The studio library, Southpark Terrace. *H.A.G.*

131. (p. 137) The Drawing-room, Southpark Terrace. *H.A.G.*

132. (p. 138) Drawing-room and studio library. *H.A.G.*

133. (p. 139) Cheval mirror in the bedroom. *H.A.G.*

134. (p. 139) The bed and fireplace. *H.A.G.*

135. (p. 140) The bedroom. Mains Street. *Annan.*

136. (p. 141) Candle-holder wall sconce, Mains Street. *Annan.*

137. (p. 141) The four-poster bed, Mains Street. *Annan.*

138. (p. 142) Artist's town house, architectural model. *G.S.A.*

139. (p. 143) Designs for an Artist's Town House. *G.S.A.*

140, 141, 142, 143, 144. (pp. 143–145) Designs for an Artist's Country Cottage. *H.A.G. 20.3 × 25 cm.*

145. (p. 145) The Daily Record Building. *H.A.G. 117 × 37.2 cm.*

146. (p. 146) Windyhill Kilmacolm. *G.S.A. 48.5 × 73.5 cm.*

147. (p. 146) Windyhill, Kilmacolm. *G.S.A. 48.5 × 73.5 cm.*

148. (p. 147) Windyhill, Kilmacolm. *Annan.*

149. (p. 148) Windyhill interior, the hall. *Annan*

150. (p. 149) Hall and staircase, Windyhill. *Annan.*

151. (p. 150) Light fittings, Windyhill. *Annan.*

152. (p. 150) Light fittings, Windyhill. *Annan.*

153. (p. 151) The Hill House, Helensburgh. *G.S.A. 33.6 × 57.2 cm.*

154. (p. 152) The Hill House. *Photograph by Ralph Burnett.*

155. (p. 153) The Hill House. *Photograph by Ralph Burnett.*

156. (p. 154) Entrance hall, Hill House. *Photograph by Ralph Burnett.*

157. (p. 155) Entrance Hall, Hill House. *Photograph by Roger Billcliffe.*

158. (p. 156) The drawing-room, Hill House. *Photograph by Ralph Burnett.*

159. (p. 157) The drawing-room, Hill House. *Photograph by Roger Billcliffe.*

160. (p. 158) The drawing-room, Hill House. *Photograph by Ralph Burnett.*

161–166 (pp. 159–163) The White Bedroom, Hill House. *Photographs by Ralph Burnett.*

167. (p. 164) The Willow Tea Rooms. *Annan.*

168. (p. 164) Menu card for White Cockade Restaurant. *G.S.A. Photograph by Roger Billcliffe. 25.2 × 31.8 cm.*

169. (p. 165) Sign for the Willow Tea Rooms. *Photograph by Ralph Burnett.*

BIBLIOGRAPHY

Anscombe, Isabelle, *A Woman's Touch: Women in Design, 1860 to the Present day*, London, Virago Press, 1984.

Billcliffe, Roger, *Charles Rennie Mackintosh: The Complete Furniture, Furniture Drawings and Interior Designs*, London, John Murrary, 1986.

Billcliffe, Roger, *Mackintosh Watercolours*, London, John Murray, 1978.

Billcliffe, Roger, *Mackintosh Textile Designs*, London, The Fine Arts Society/John Murray, 1982.

Billcliffe, Roger, *Architectural Sketches and Flower Drawings by Charles Rennie Mackintosh*, London, Academy Editions, 1977.

Buchanan, William. ed., *Mackintosh's Masterwork, The Glasgow School of Art*, Glasgow, Richard Drew, 1989.

Cooper, Jackie, *Mackintosh Architecture*, London, Academy Editions, 1984.

Howarth, Thomas, *Charles Rennie Mackintosh and the Modern Movement*, London, Routledge and Kegan Paul, 1977.

Jones, Anthony. ed., *Charles Rennie Mackintosh*, Essays and catalogue for touring exhibition, Japan, 1984, Tokyo, Japan Art and Culture Association/Isetan and Daimaru Museums, 1984.

Kimura, Hiroaki and Macmillan, Andrew, *Charles Rennie Mackintosh, Process Architecture Series, Number 50*, Tokyo, Process Architecture Publishing Co., 1984.

Larner, Gerald and Celia, *The Glasgow Style*, London, Paul Harris, 1979.

Macleod, Robert, *Charles Rennie Mackintosh: Architect and Artist*, Glasgow, Collins and Son, 1983.

Miller, A. and Opfer, J., *Charles Rennie Mackintosh's Scotland Street School: A New Survey*, Glasgow, Glasgow Print Studio, 1982.

Moffat, Alistair, *Remembering Charles Rennie Mackintosh*, Lanark, Colin Baxter, 1989.

Nuttgens, Patrick. ed., *Mackintosh and his Contemporaries*, London, John Murray, 1988.

Pevsner, Nikolaus, *Pioneers of Modern Design*, London, Penguin Books, 1984.

Varnedoe, Kirk, *Vienna 1900: Art Architecture and Design*, New York, Museum of Modern Art, 1986.

Young, Andrew McLaren, *Charles Rennie Mackintosh: Architecture Design and Planning*, The Edinburgh Festival 1968, catalogue of exhibition Edinburgh, Scottish Arts Council and the Edinburgh Festival Society, 1968.

MACKINTOSH INDEX